Presented by
Evelyn Kyle

# ONE TO EIGHT

J. N. BARNETTE

# ONE TO EIGHT

J. N. BARNETTE



The Sunday School Board of the Southern Baptist Convention
Nashville, Tennessee

*Printed in the United States of America*
100.AL54B.Co.

## DIRECTIONS FOR THE TEACHING AND STUDY OF THIS BOOK FOR CREDIT

### I. *Directions for the Teacher*

1. Ten class periods of forty-five minutes each, or the equivalent, are required for the completion of a book for credit.

2. The teacher is given, when requested, an award on the book taught.

3. The teacher shall give a written examination covering the subject matter in the textbook. The examination may take the form of assigned work to be done between the class sessions, in the class sessions, or as a final examination.

*Exception:* All who attend all of the class sessions; who read the book through by the close of the course; and who, in the judgment of the teacher, do the classwork satisfactorily may be exempted from taking the examination.

4. Application for Sunday school awards should be sent to the state Sunday school department, where forms may be secured on which to make application for awards. These forms should be made in triplicate. Keep the last copy for the church file, and send the other two copies.

### II. *Directions for the Student**

(*The student must be fifteen years of age or older to receive Sunday school credit.)

1. In Classwork

(1) The student must attend at least six of the ten forty-five minute class periods to be entitled to take the class examination.

(2) The student must certify that the textbook has been read. (In rare cases where students may find it impracticable to read the book before the completion of the classwork, the teacher may accept a promise to read the book carefully within the next two weeks. This applies only to students who do the written work.)

(3) The student must take a written examination, making a minimum grade of 70 per cent, or qualify according to *Exception* noted above.

2. In Individual Study by Correspondence

Those who for any reason wish to study the book without the guidance of a teacher will use one of the following methods:

(1) Write answers to the questions printed in the book, or

(2) Write a development of the chapter outlines.

In either case the student must read the book through.

Students may find profit in studying the text together, but where awards are requested, individual papers are required.

All written work done by such students on books for Sunday school credit should be sent to the state Sunday school secretary.

NOTE—This book is in Section II of the Sunday School Training Course, and diploma credit will be given for its study during 1954-1955.

# CONTENTS

# 1. WHAT DO WE MEAN—ONE TO EIGHT?

We hope the title has made you curious—and even interested to know what this book is about. It deals with the central work of a church, evangelism. It approaches that from a practical point of view and with the eager, expectant hope that thousands of our churches may be helped to reap a greater harvest of souls through the years ahead.

*One to Eight* represents a degree of success in evangelism which should be realized, on the average, by Southern Baptist churches—that is, year by year we should be able to report one baptism for every eight church members. At present the record shows approximately one baptism for every twenty church members. This ratio of baptisms to church members has remained about the same for our Convention as a whole for many years. Growing numbers of churches, however, have increased their baptisms to a great degree—many of them baptizing people at the rate of one for every ten, eight, six, five, and even two church members.

How these churches have succeeded in achieving such results, and what lessons all of our churches may learn from them, is the burden of this book. *One to Eight* is a dream—yes, but a dream founded upon the compassion of Christ, the command of our Father, the successful achievement of many churches, and the sincere desire of every pastor and Christian worker—that more lost people shall be won to Christ year by year.

It is our prayer that in this study we may be caught by the challenge of the practical use of the Sunday school forces, the Bible-teaching function of the church, to win lost multitudes to Christ "while it is day: the night cometh, when no man can work."

## I. Ratio of Baptists to Church Members Alarming

*"Why is it that our church wins only one person to Christ for every twenty church members each year? What is wrong?" This question, presented by a young man to his pastor, focuses our attention on a serious condition in our churches.*

The statisticians tell us that there are more than 30,000,000 people nine years of age and up in the territory where Southern Baptist churches are located who are not Christians. Reports show 8,000,000 Southern Baptists whose names are carried on the church rolls. The ratio of baptisms to church members in the 30,000 Southern Baptist churches shows an annual average of one baptism for every twenty members. Thirty million and more lost people in our church communities and 8,000,000 who belong to missionary Baptist churches, and our churches report an annual average ratio of baptisms to church members of one to twenty!

Immediately your question is, "Where does my church stand in this general average of baptisms to church members?" You can easily find the answer to that question. Write down the number of church members you reported in your last letter to the annual associational meeting and divide by the number of baptisms reported in the same letter. The answer will give you the number of church members for each baptism reported. For this check do not use the number of "resident members" or the number of "active members." Use the exact number of people reported in your last letter to your association.

The ratio in the churches varies from one baptism for every two members to as few as one for every 150 members. The average, however, is one to twenty. Is your church above or below the Convention average?

Will you further examine the question: Why does it take a church an entire year to report just one baptism for every twenty or forty or seventy of her own church members?

## II. Why the Wide Variation in the Churches?

Why do some churches report one baptism for every two church members, while others report one for every seventy church members? The answer to this question will reveal that many factors are involved, and we do not mean to say that every church can have a ratio of one baptism for every eight church members. We all share the conviction, however, that all the churches working together must seek to win more people to Christ so that the ratio of all Southern Baptist churches will be changed from one to *twenty* to one to *eight.*

One answer advanced as to why the ratio of baptisms to church members varies in the churches is that there is a higher percentage of lost people in some communities than in others. This is certainly true. Does this fact, however, necessarily determine the number of baptisms in a church? Reports do not so indicate. There are lost people in almost every community.

One superintendent reports that when a census was suggested, he and other workers replied, "No need for a census here; we know by name every person in this community." A census was made and revealed the names of sixty-three people nine years of age and above who were not Christians and who were not known by the Sunday school superintendent or the teachers. The sixty-three people were not the only unsaved people in the community. They were the ones not known by the leaders. This condition was discovered in an average rural church community.

In towns and cities the number of lost people would, in most communities, be much greater. It is possible that in some communities there are very few lost people. But without a thorough survey no one would want to accept finally the statement, "There are no lost people here."

Moreover, a church is not necessarily confined to one location in the task of winning people to the Lord. A church may have work in two or a dozen locations scattered over a wide area. Suppose a church should win all the lost people in a community. Does that excuse a church from the obligation to witness "in Samaria, and unto the uttermost part of the earth"?

The question keeps pressing in: Why should our churches keep on and on reporting just one baptism for every twenty church members?

What is the real cause back of the wide variation in the churches in the ratio of baptisms to church members? Facts reveal that, perhaps more than at any other point, the answer is found in the comparative level of the Sunday school enrolment to the total church membership. All reports in our Convention show that the majority of people are won to Christ after they have been enrolled in Sunday school.

It follows that when the Sunday school enrolment is greater than the total church membership, the soul-winning opportunity of a church is increased in that proportion. All reports show that a rapidly growing Sunday school enrolment increases the number of baptisms in a church, while a static Sunday school enrolment reduces the number greatly.

It should be said here that the preaching service is central. The purpose of this study is to show that by the use of the Sunday school a church can provide for the preaching service a maximum soul-winning opportunity that is centered in Bible teaching. There would be very few public professions of faith in Christ if it were not for the preaching service. On the other hand, there are very few professions of faith in churches that do not have Sunday schools. So it is not one or the other. The Sunday school to enrol the people and teach the Bible, and the preaching service to lead to public profession, are both essential in a Bible-centered, soul-winning program.

For an example, here is the record as taken from the associational minutes in a number of associations. These associations are located in several of the states and involve approximately 300 churches. These churches are located in open country, villages, towns, and cities. They are typical of Southern Baptist churches generally.

The record of these churches involves a period of five years or more. Many churches show good records for one year, but when a period of five or more years is studied, the records may be quite different. Five consecutive years or more of achievements in a church indicate possibilities of permanency in the rate of achievements. Let us examine the table on the next page to see if it reveals a relationship between Sunday school enrolment and baptisms.

Reading the first line of the following table, we see that when a group of churches has 170 or more people in Sunday school for every 100 names on the church books, they have the conditions which result in one baptism for every 4.5 church members.

Reading the last line, we see that when a group of churches has only 30 to 39 people enrolled in Sunday school for every 100 names on the church roll, the result is that in such churches it takes, on the average, 70 members a whole year to win one person.

### How the Sunday School Enrolment Relates to Baptisms

| *When the average Sunday school enrolment for every 100 church members is:* | *Then the ratio for baptisms to church members is:* |
|---|---|
| 170 or more | 1 to 4.5 |
| 160—169 | 1 to 8 |
| 150—159 | 1 to 9.7 |
| 140—149 | 1 to 11.4 |
| 130—139 | 1 to 12.4 |
| 120—129 | 1 to 13 |
| 110—119 | 1 to 16 |
| 100—109 | 1 to 19.6 |
| 90— 99 | 1 to 21 |
| 80— 89 | 1 to 23.4 |
| 70— 79 | 1 to 24.5 |
| 60— 69 | 1 to 27 |
| 50— 59 | 1 to 33 |
| 40— 49 | 1 to 52 |
| 30— 39 | 1 to 70 |

It may be true that another group of churches selected from another group of associations would show some variations in percentages and ratios. There are many factors that enter into the number of baptisms a church will report year by year. It is true, however, that any survey made, including one year or a number of years, has shown that the growth of the Sunday school has more to do with the number of baptisms than any combination of all other factors. Dr. E. Hermond Westmoreland, pastor of the South Main Baptist Church, Houston, Texas, says out of his experience that "the increase in additions to the church will be in direct proportion to the growth of the Sunday school."

While the table just studied shows that the relation

of the Sunday school enrolment to the church membership has a decided bearing on the number of baptisms, it does not reveal all the facts. The rate of growth of a Sunday school has a direct bearing on the number of baptisms in a church. The greater the growth of a Sunday school, the greater are the soul-winning opportunities of a church.

The purpose of this study, therefore, is clear: to show how Southern Baptist churches can change the ratio of baptisms to church members from the present average of one to twenty to one to eight by bringing the Sunday school enrolment to exceed by 25 per cent the total church membership, and by enlisting the entire church membership in the Training Union. On the basis of the present church membership this would increase the present annual number of baptisms from about 350,000 each year to 1,000,000 each year. The question for churches to face and settle is, Can this average be attained?

## III. Many Churches Have Good Ratio of Baptisms to Church Membership

The church at Energy, Illinois, in 1951 baptized one person for every five church members. In 1952 this church baptized one person for every six church members. In 1953 the ratio was one baptism for every seven church members. At the present time the church membership is 325, while the Sunday school enrolment is 459. There is nothing unusual about the community, people, or conditions at Energy, except that the spirit and work are unusual.

Allapattah Baptist Church in Miami, Florida, has a record of one baptism for every eleven church members for the past eight-year period. In 1953 this church baptized 360 people, and the average number of baptisms for each of the eight consecutive years is 275. The average number of baptisms per Sunday for the eight consecutive years is five. The average annual gain in Sunday school enrolment for the eight years has been 253.

Murray Hill Baptist Church in Jacksonville, Florida, has a record of one baptism for every eleven church members for a seventeen-year period. The present Sunday school enrolment is 2,412, while the total church membership is 1,623. The annual average net Sunday school enrolment gain for seventeen years has been 135.

### IV. All Churches Can Better the Ratio of Baptisms to Church Membership

Some churches could change their ratio from one to sixty to one to twenty. A ratio of one to twenty may be excellent in some churches. Another group of churches could change the ratio from one to twenty to one to ten. Still another group could change the ratio from one to fifteen to one to eight. Another group of churches could change their ratio from one to ten to one to five, or in some churches even one to three. Achievements in numbers of churches are sufficient to indicate that Southern Baptist churches can change the ratio for the entire Convention from one to twenty to one to eight. Would you like for your church to have a part in such an undertaking?

We come now to study how your church and my church can change the ratio of baptisms to church members. There are six factors that will contribute to the achievement of this important improvement. All six of these factors will have to be present in a church, first in the hearts and practices of the leaders and then in the lives of the church membership as a whole.

### 1. *Impelling Desire to See People Saved*

Do you honestly desire to change the ratio of baptisms to church membership in your church? Can you sincerely say in substance what Paul said, "My heart's desire and prayer to God is that my own people may be saved"? This desire must be stronger than any combination of all other desires.

The story given by Jesus of the man who found a pearl of great price brings us to the very heart of this important matter. When the man found the pearl of great price, he immediately disposed of all other matters and invested all he had in the one supreme matter. Are you willing to do just that in this important business of winning the lost people to Christ?

A lovely woman was requested to build a class of girls, some of them not Christians. Her reply was, "I have accepted so many obligations outside of my church that I cannot possibly take on any more work." Could it be that a part in a woman's club can have a stronger pull on the heart of a Christian woman than the salvation of lost people in her immediate community? Time is found for that which we value most highly.

A church last year invested $10,000 in remodeling the fellowship hall. This expenditure of money at least postponed any provision for Bible study and Christian training. The question here is not in any way concerned with whether or not a fellowship hall is a good thing. The question goes far deeper than that and deals with what shall have priority in the provision and work of a church.

Fellowship halls are no doubt profitable and desirable. But the question here is, Which should come first, Bible study and New Testament evangelism, or recreational facilities? What is the "heart's desire" of your church? Of your class? Of your group?

### 2. *Willingness to Do Whatever Is Necessary*

The University Baptist Church in Coral Gables, Florida, moved in three years from 12 Sunday school departments to 21, from 46 Sunday school classes to 94. The results show a net Sunday school enrolment gain from 694 to 1,625, and the number of baptisms from 26 in 1949 to 167 in 1953. In 1949 the ratio of baptisms to church members was one to thirty-one. In 1953 the ratio was one to 8.8.

The pastor, Ralph H. Langley, says: "When I saw that Sunday school growth and the number of baptisms in the church have such a vital relationship, I became not only willing but determined to organize more Sunday school departments and classes, to provide a plan of visitation, to train our Sunday school workers, and to use the Sunday school as I had never used it before. The results have convinced me that a pastor and a church can win more people to Christ Jesus, train them, hold them, and enlist them by use of the Sunday school and Training Union than through any other means now known to our churches. In taking this position, a pastor does not surrender the leadership of the church to outside agencies. He does organize the entire church membership for Bible teaching, for training, and for work. I preach to many more people since our Sunday school has been growing."

The use of the Sunday school in the University Baptist Church is emphasized because the program used in the church shows the extra, out-beyond fruits that always come when a church uses the Sunday school and Training Union to put all the church to work in the enlistment of people and in the training of all the church members.

3. *A Program of Sunday School Growth*

It will be profitable to go back to a study of conditions in the churches studied earlier in this chapter. Notice that the churches with an average of 170 and up in Sunday school for every 100 church members report an average of one baptism for every 4.5 church members. Churches that reported 30 to 39 in Sunday school for every 100 church members report an average of one baptism for every seventy church members. Every general survey made shows beyond any doubt that Sunday school growth and baptisms in a church go along together.

Every Sunday school can be made to grow. A church can use the Sunday school to enrol people regularly week by week and month by month. Some Sunday schools may grow much faster than others because of a number of reasons. Any Sunday school, however, can be made to grow, either in the present location or in branch Sunday schools in various locations. Two examples are given as proof of these statements.

The first one is from a very small church in the open country in Alabama. The Sunday school enrolment in 1946 was 23 as reported in the associational minutes. The report was about the same in 1952. In 1953 this church produced a net gain in Sunday school of 78, which brought the Sunday school enrolment from 23 to 101. The number of baptisms in 1946 was zero. In 1953 the number of baptisms was 19.

What had happened? The church had been in the community for years. The population in the community had increased through the years. There had been one class for all Adults. This condition had existed for many years. But not until the church organized four classes for Adults and additional classes and departments for other groups, conducted two or three training schools, and the pastor and superintendent began to visit and lead the people to visit for Sunday school enrolment, did the people attend. Now there are three times as many in the preaching services as formerly. The weekly offerings have increased five times, and one person has been baptized for every four church members. There are 10,000 and more churches in the Convention that can experience similar gains when the laws of Sunday school growth are applied.

Let us consider the record of a large church located in the heart of a great city. For five years this church lost in Sunday school enrolment. The number of baptisms for a five-year period totaled 680, which was an average of 136. Several years ago, this church began to organize new departments and classes and to train workers. The reported Sunday school enrolment in 1953 was greater by 1,240 than it was in 1949. The total number of baptisms for the period 1949-1953 was 1,323, or an average of 265 per year. Thus this church changed the ratio from one to fifty-five to one to thirty-four by changing the loss in Sunday school enrolment to an average annual gain of 248 for the past five years.

Some few churches may find that the number of unenrolled people in the immediate church community is limited. Every such church can find a needy location and organize a branch Sunday school. Do you question that statement? It may be possible that not every church will find a place in its own association to organize a branch Sunday school. If so, what can these churches do to make the Sunday school grow? If yours is such a church, there is a way.

Locate some Baptist family from your church, or some other church in your association, now living in some other state, in some community where there is not a Southern Baptist Sunday school. Work through the state mission department in the state involved and through your Baptist family, and organize and build a Sunday school and a church.

The Sunday school can begin in the home of the Baptist family. This has been done, it is being done now, and your church can do it. Your pastor or some worker authorized by the home church will visit this family, conduct a revival meeting, and advise with those in the new work and the home church as to the right provision for the new work. Of course, the church would pay the expenses of the pastor.

4. *A Long-range Program of Evangelism*

Improving the baptism ratio calls for a long-range program of evangelism. How can such a program be planned? The population report shows that there are 11,500,000 babies under four years of age now living in the nation. The report from the various religious bodies shows that four out of five of these babies are not enrolled in any Sunday school. One enrolled, four not enrolled! Southern Baptist churches could, without much doubt, enrol one million or more of these babies in one year's time, an average of 33 per church.

The vital statistics as reported by the Federal Government show that in 1953 more than 4,000,000 babies were born in this nation. Reports in the early part of 1954 indicate that the birth rate will be as high in 1954 as in 1953. It is possible for Southern Baptist churches in one year to enrol 800,000 or more of the babies that will be born during the year.

Suppose the churches should enrol 800,000 babies during this Sunday school year and as soon as possible transfer them to the Nursery departments in the church buildings and provide classes for the parents of these babies? It is possible to keep most of these

800,000 children in Sunday school year after year.

Now look at the years ahead. Soon these children will be older Primaries and then Juniors. You will find there a soul-winning opportunity of approximately 800,000 in number every year, provided we enrol the babies year by year as they are born and then make provision for them and their parents in our Sunday schools. Herein is a long-range soul-winning opportunity of a permanent nature. It is possible and surely it is right.

5. *One or More Branch Stations*

Branch stations are fully discussed in chapter 6. The need for branch stations is placed here because it belongs in the list of things a church can do to increase the number of baptisms.

6. *A Controlling Purpose*

A church has a central task around which all other activities must find their place. What is that central task? We go to the New Testament for the answer. One of the clearest statements of the purpose of Jesus in the world is found in Luke 19:10, "For the Son of man is come to seek and to save that which was lost." Over and over, Jesus tried to deposit this truth in the hearts of his followers so that they would know and feel beyond any doubt that his purpose was not to establish an earthly kingdom but to save the souls and lives of people.

Before Jesus ascended to the Father, he called his followers together and committed to them this central task. One of the clearest statements of it is found in John 20:21, "As my Father hath sent me, even so send I you."

His disciples did come to understand that their one

task in the world was the proclamation of the gospel of the Lord Jesus Christ. Hear Peter and the others as they speak to the Jewish authorities, "We cannot but speak the things which we have seen and heard." Hear John as he affirms, "But these are written, that ye might believe that Jesus is the Christ, the Son of God; and that believing ye might have life through his name." Hear Paul as he says, "Woe is unto me, if I preach not the gospel!"

Men and women ask questions about the work done in the churches. They have the right to be given the correct answers to these questions. One of the most often repeated questions is "Why?" It takes many forms and deals with practical matters. Why take a census? Why erect another building? Why organize more classes? Why visit every week? Why study books and attend meetings? Why grade on the age basis? Why promote Young People and Adults every year? Why should we sing "When I Survey the Wondrous Cross" for a special on Sunday morning? Why should we have evangelistic services on Sunday morning? Give men and women satisfying answers to these questions and you will increase the number of baptisms in your church. Why? Because churches that do these things have Sunday schools that grow faster. Churches that have rapidly growing Sunday schools win more people.

A man of mature years gave a satisfying answer to the question of "Why" on a Sunday morning in 1931.

It was in the First Baptist Church of Bartlesville, Oklahoma. The church had been engaged in an eight-day Sunday school enlargement campaign. A census had been taken; plans had been made for many new classes and several new departments; partitions had been placed in some of the larger classrooms to make provision for new departments.

On the second Sunday morning the people came together in the church auditorium, and the enlarged plans were presented. Presently a man who had not been in any of the conferences arose and asked the question, "Why?" His statements ran something like this: "Why do you want to disturb us? We are happy and contented as we are. Why do you want to disturb our class? We love our teacher and we like things just as they are."

There were a number of amens from people who had not been present during the week. After a painful period of silence a man with hair as white as snow stood and asked for the privilege of saying a word. He restated the question, "Why all these changes and adjustments?" and he answered in this way: "Years ago we went down by the riverside and put up a small one-room church building and finally paid for it through the personal sacrifices of many of the members. Why did we do it? Because somebody was lost. A few years passed; we erected this church building. We are still trying to pay for it. Why? Because somebody was lost. Why did you take a census last Sunday? Why are you suggesting these new classes and these new departments? Why have you disturbed these men and women who have been contented in the classes as they are? Fellow church members, I am quite sure I have the answer. All this has been done because somebody today is lost."

The old man took his seat. The pastor waited. There were tears in the eyes of some of the people. Presently the pastor asked the question, "What shall we do?" They knew what they wanted to do. Every man and every woman present went as the church had suggested, because they, too, had found a satisfying answer to all their questions.

It is all for evangelism, winning people's souls and lives to Christ. All good Sunday school work results in evangelism. This conception does not minimize any other phase of work in a church. It does place bringing people to Jesus for salvation and teaching them to observe all things taught by him in the central place accorded it by the New Testament.

### Questions for Review

1. What is the significance of the title *One to Eight?*
2. What is the most evident explanation for the wide variation in churches in the ratio of baptisms to church members?
3. Name six essentials which a church must have in order to better its ratio for baptisms.

# 2. ADULTS CAN BE WON

Large numbers of adults can be won to Jesus Christ, church membership, and Christian service.

Our failure to win large numbers of unsaved people in the past is not an adequate proof that adults cannot be won. Neither is our present failure to win large numbers of men and women sufficient reason to excuse us from efforts to win adults. Have we done all things possible to win them? It may be that the first essential step in winning adults is a change of attitude. Should churches believe that Jesus will save adults? Do churches actually believe that it is possible to win people after they reach the twenty-fifth year? The examples of the past and the examples of the present convince us that adults can be won.

## I. Adults Have Been Won

It is both a matter of history and current experience that adults have been won to a saving faith in Jesus Christ.

### 1. *Jesus Won Adults*

Jesus began his ministry by winning men. He started with Andrew and Peter. He invited them to follow him. They accepted his invitation. He called James and John, and they accepted his call and followed him.

### 2. *The Early Disciples Won Adults*

Peter and the others won a multitude of adults on the day of Pentecost. Paul and Barnabas won men and women at Antioch. Likewise they won adults and established churches on their missionary journeys.

### 3. *Churches Are Winning Adults Today*

Churches today are winning and using adults. In this respect there has been a marked change in recent years.

Mr. A. V. Washburn gives a splendid statement of this fact.

"Back at the turn of the century a survey reported the peak years at which conversion and baptism occured as follows: In the first place, sixteen to seventeen years of age; next, twelve to thirteen years of age; and next, ten years of age.

"Fifty years ago, the number of Adult baptisms evidently was so limited as not to be included. A recent survey in Southern Baptist churches, made some three or four years ago by Dr. Porter Routh, indicated these figures: The Junior years led, reporting 30 per cent of the baptisms, and I believe the top year was the twelfth year. But the next largest number of baptisms came in the Adult years, reporting 25 per cent of the total baptisms.

"Now what has happened in these intervening years from the turn of the century until now which has brought about such a change? Certainly one of the significant developments has been the growth in the Adult program in the Sunday school, which has brought tens of thousands of unsaved men and women under the influence of the teaching of God's Word and the preaching of the gospel. It is a matter of common observation that where Adult Sunday school classes are growing, Adults in great numbers are being won to Christ, but where there is a static Adult enrolment, few Adults are won."

Here is a testimony from Dr. Homer G. Lindsay, pastor of the First Baptist Church, Jacksonville, Florida. This church is located in the heart of a big, busy city, with all the problems of such churches. Fifteen years ago, this church faced the future with inadequate space and almost every conceivable problem that a church could have. Hear the testimony of the pastor:

"In the past fourteen years the First Baptist Church of Jacksonville, Florida, has baptized 2,170 people, an average of 155 a year. Thirty-four per cent of those baptized, or 740, were Adults. This is an annual average of 53 Adults for the fourteen years.

"I think the fact that 34 per cent of our total baptisms are Adults is evidence that the Adults can be won to Christ. That one of every three persons I baptize is an Adult may be attributed in large measure to the provision we have made for them in the Sunday school. We have five graded Adult departments and observe Promotion Day annually. Our facilities for these Adults are on a par with the facilities we provide for the rest of the Sunday school.

"Four of the Adult superintendents are outstanding deacons of our church, and the fifth is the pastor's wife. Our Adult teachers are some of the finest members in the church. They are regular in their attendance and faithful in their support of the training schools. Our church was seventh in the Convention last year in total training awards.

"We have a conviction that you must train for what you would have your church to be. I personally teach three or four Adult courses each year. In teaching the soul-winning books, we always reserve Thursday night for assigned soul-winning visitation and practical suggestions on how to deal with the problems to be encountered.

"We encourage our Adults to use their class organization in both regular visitation and soul-winning visitation. It is rare that an Adult stays very long in a class without confessing Christ and coming into the church. Our teachers are never satisfied until they see their pupils won to full allegiance to Christ.

"We have churchwide days of visitation, but most all our Adult classes have their own regular weekly nights to visit.

"We strive to keep our classes small enough for the teacher to visit and for them to have a wonderful fellowship by knowing each other. We consider fifteen to twenty to be an ideal number for an Adult class. We keep multiplying our classes so that we can give more individual attention. With such personal attention it is much easier for the teacher to win the lost pupils to Christ.

"It is not an unusual sight to see an Adult teacher walking the aisle with a pupil coming to confess Christ. To win one Adult to Christ usually means the winning of several members of a family, or even a whole family, to Christ.

"It takes much personal work to win most Adults to Christ, and herein is the importance of having small, graded classes of Adults. It is important for the teacher to know the members personally and individually. It is also important for the teacher to enlist the concern of the saved members of the class. The Christians grow as they manifest their concern in personal work and visitation.

"The right kind of Sunday school work with Adults will win Adults to Christ. We have averaged baptizing three converts per Sunday for nearly fourteen years, and one of every three was an Adult."

Here is a testimony from Dr. Robert S. Scales, pastor of the Trinity Baptist Church in Oklahoma City:

"Adults can be won. During a recent associational year the church of which I was pastor baptized 189 persons, of whom 105 were Adults. Ninety per cent of these Adults were enrolled in the Sunday school before they were won to the Lord.

"My personal conviction is that these results came from an enlarged and a closely graded organization that brought about an intensive drive for the enlistment of more Adults, coupled with the close personal touch which the pupils had with the teachers and the other members of the classes.

"For five years I was pastor of a church which had one large Bible class for all the men. During that time I baptized only a very small number of men. During the next four years in another pastorate we increased our Adult organization from one department to three, from two men's classes to eight, and I baptized 800 persons, of whom a very unusually great percentage were men.

"During the first two years of my present pastorate we have increased our Adult organization from four departments to seven, with a corresponding number of new classes. Where we had practically no unchurched Adults enrolled, we are gradually building up a great group of evangelistic possibilities. It is the only way."

Here is a testimony from the experience of Dr. J. Gilbert Hutchinson, pastor of the First Baptist Church, Clanton, Alabama. Clanton is a typical county seat town made up of people who are "the salt of the earth." Clanton has all the conservatism that is usually evident in such towns. Hear the testimony from Dr. Hutchinson:

"During the period 1940 to 1949 our church had an average of 15 baptisms per year. Since 1949 this average has increased to 55 per year. However, the average of Adults baptized since 1949 has been 18 per year, which is more than the previous ten-year average for the whole Sunday school. We find that our Sunday school is our best evangelistic agency, not only for Juniors, but for Adults as well.

"The plan which we have used at the First Baptist Church, Clanton, Alabama, has produced wonderful results. We have followed the Sunday school plan of Southern Baptist churches and herewith testify to the worthiness of this program. The steps which follow look simple, but in the light of our results we feel they are profound: provide space for the Adults, grade and promote them, give them good officers and teachers, and train them to attend the preaching service.

"Of course, Adults can be won. Christ gives us the power to do it according to his promise. Many men and women did respond to his invitation."

Here is a copy of a letter received from Dr. C. E. Autrey, a member of the evangelistic staff of the Home Mission Board:

Dear Mr. Barnette:

I just received a letter from Dr. E. Paul Fisher, pastor of the Kensington Avenue Baptist Church, Kansas City, Missouri, in which he said the following:

"On May 10, previous to the revival, we reorganized our Sunday school, moving up from thirteen departments to thirty departments. With such a great enlargement we needed to enlist 100 new workers, and all of them came from the Adults of our Sunday school. In spite of the fact that we took 100 workers from the Adults, we have an Adult enrolment now of approximately the same as we had before we graded, and this in less than ten months since we graded.

"It was interesting to me to note in a study of the people who came into our church during the revival in November that 70 of them were Adults and that every one of them was enrolled in our Sunday school. As a matter of fact, I do not know of a single one of the 116 who united with our church during the revival in November who was not in Sunday school. I suppose this is unusual, but to me it is remarkable and just proof to me again that the Sunday school is the evangelical agency of our church.

"In January and February, 1954, we took a complete every-member canvass. Last year we had pledged to our church $31,000. Now we have $70,000 pledged and feel confident that we will close the year with a total income of $80,000. This kind of results could not have been accomplished without our Sunday school enlargement nor without our wonderful revival."

I trust you can use this testimony from Dr. E. Paul Fisher, in whose church it was my privilege to conduct a revival last fall.

Sincerely,
C. E. Autrey

## II. There Are Many Adults Yet to Be Won

There are 18,000,000 men and women twenty-five years of age and above in the territory where Southern Baptist churches are located who are not Christians.

A census by a church in North Carolina revealed 1,016 Adult possibilities. Of this number 295 were unsaved and 210 were unaffiliated Baptists. In a rural community in North Carolina 214 Adult possibilities were discovered and 75 of them were unsaved and 47 were unaffiliated Baptists.

In a small community in South Carolina 166 Adult possibilities were found and 59 of them were unsaved.

There are unsaved men and women in every community. Why are there so many unsaved adults today? There are perhaps a number of reasons.

### 1. *Today's Adults Not Won When Children*

A rather typical example comes out of experience.

In 1924 a religious census in a town of about 1,500 people revealed eight Junior boys and girls in the Baptist Sunday school, and forty-seven not in any Sunday school. There was one class for the Juniors, with an average attendance of about five. A Junior department with eight classes was organized, and in twelve months forty-seven Juniors were enrolled in that Baptist Sunday school. None of the parents of these Juniors were in Sunday school. Classes were started for Adults, and many of these were enlisted along with the Juniors.

Up until 1925 to 1930 very meager provision had been made in the Sunday school even for the children. It was as late as 1925 before there were more than two or three churches that had more than one department for Juniors. Now there are churches that have eight departments for Juniors alone.

It was as late as 1945 before many churches had any adequate provision in the church building for the babies. Now there are churches with as many as twelve Nursery departments. In addition, some churches have four or more Cradle Roll departments enrolling the babies who do not attend.

There was a time when it was difficult to find more than one class for the Primaries, Juniors, or Intermediates in any of the churches in the open country. Today many of these beautiful churches have departments for each age group.

Many adults are unsaved today because churches failed to win the children twenty-five to sixty years ago.

### 2. *Meager Provision for Adults in the Past*

Forty years ago, adults were not really expected to attend Sunday school. This conception resulted in very meager, if any, provision in the church building or in the organization for men and women.

The organized class movement grew up outside the churches. However, we owe much to the popular organized class movement. It revealed to the churches great possibilities for good. There were some definite weaknesses in the movement. It was not church-centered. The chief purpose was fellowship, which rapidly tended toward social implications only. While the units were called "Bible Classes," there was usually very little Bible study or Bible teaching.

The churches were compelled to take over these situations which so vitally affected their Adults. It has been a long, difficult period of changing from independent, class-centered groups to church-related groups. It has been difficult to change from a popular lecture by the so-called "teacher" to Bible study by the class members, planned, directed, and shared by one who really teaches.

There were exceptions, of course, but not many of the independent classes won large numbers of people to Christ. After a few years a static condition usually developed. These classes were filled with church members, often including from three to six denominations. These church members had not been trained by the churches or by the classes to major on winning the lost. So it soon developed that there was no room for lost people in the classes. This condition resulted in much activity by these classes, but most of it was visiting each other, or planning and presenting programs on Sunday morning which were pitched on the entertainment level.

All of this contributed to the ultimate disintegration of the classes. Gradually these big, independent classes dissolved. A few have held the enrolment to near former figures. Very few have increased in numbers over their enrolment of twenty-five years ago.

3. *Soul-winning Efforts of Past Confined to Annual Revival*

The annual revivals have been an important factor in evangelism, and Southern Baptists praise the Lord for the revival meetings. However, the annual revivals were not enough. They did not win many adults.

4. *No Program of Conservation Prevailed*

Up until two decades ago, churches were slow to have Training Unions. Very few churches had any sort of plan for training church members. Twenty-five years ago it was unusual for a church to have a training school of any kind to train the Sunday school workers. The result is 3,000,000 unenlisted church members today. A careful survey will show near 100 per cent enlistment of new converts during the past ten years in churches that have had good Training Unions and a plan to train Sunday school officers and teachers.

## III. Churches of Today Are Providing for and Winning Adults

Space for Adults and organization for Adults are never questioned in planning new church buildings today, but it is still difficult really to provide adequately for Adults.

1. *Additional Classes and Departments Are Reaching Adults*

The churches in the beautiful countrysides are organizing departments for Adults, with a class for every fifteen to twenty available men, and, of course, a similar provision for women.

Larger churches are organizing multiple departments for Adults, until today one church already has nine departments with 56 classes, and other churches are planning in the buildings for two, four, six, eight, ten, and even twelve departments with as high as 65 or more classes. Have these changes produced fruit? In 1943 the total number of Adults enrolled in Southern Baptist schools was 1,166,552. In 1953 the enrolment of Adults was 2,597,367, or more than twice as many as ten years ago.

### 2. *The Group Plan Is Ideal for Using Adults to Win Adults*

This plan is not presented as a "Sunday school" program. It is presented as a church plan, implemented through the Sunday school.

What is the group plan for a class of Adults?

The class is divided into groups, at the beginning, with four members and a group leader. Each group leader is given regularly the names of one or two prospects for his group. It is his responsibility to use the members of his group who are Christians to help him enlist these prospects.

After the prospects have been enrolled as members of the class, the next step is to win them to an acceptance of Christ and then to church membership. The next step is to enlist those who are members of the church to help reach others.

It would be the duty of the teacher, department superintendent, pastor, and general superintendent to encourage the growth of the class by keeping the groups small enough to permit growth. When the group has an enrolment of eight or nine, two groups should be formed.

When several of the groups have earned the privilege and recognition of making two groups from the one, another class should be started. Unless new groups and new classes are started, the growth will cease. When growth stops, soul-winning will practically stop.

How better could a church be organized for adult soul-winning, enlistment, giving, and serving, than with a sufficient number of Sunday school classes functioning on the group basis?

Look for a moment at what would happen if all the groups in all the classes should get hold of what is possible in using Adults, and then do something about it. There are approximately 100,000 Sunday school classes for Adults in the 30,000 Southern Baptist churches. There is, or should be, a minimum average of three groups to a class. This, as you quickly see, totals 300,000 groups. Now, see what will result when these groups average winning two persons each this year, and then each succeeding year. The total would be 600,000 Adults alone. Is such an achievement beyond realization?

Could your group win at least two people to Christ in a year, provided your church, through your pastor, superintendent, and others, would encourage you, train you, provide you with the prospects, help you when necessary? Surely you could and would. This is one significant way for Southern Baptist churches to reach a one to eight ratio in baptisms.

## IV. A New Testament Example: Four Men Bring a Man to Jesus

Luke gives us a striking example of how men or

women can win adults. It is an extreme example. It is recorded in Luke 5:18-26:

And, behold, men brought in a bed a man which was taken with a palsy: and they sought means to bring him in, and to lay him before him. And when they could not find by what way they might bring him in because of the multitude, they went upon the house top, and let him down through the tiling with his couch into the midst before Jesus. And when he saw their faith, he said unto him, Man, thy sins are forgiven thee. . . . I say unto thee, Arise, and take up thy couch, and go into thine house. And immediately he rose up before them, and took up that whereon he lay, and departed to his own house, glorifying God. And they were all amazed, and they glorified God, and were filled with fear, saying, We have seen strange things to day.

No doubt this example is given that men and women everywhere may see that it is possible to win difficult cases to Jesus Christ. It is made so wonderfully clear that Christ is ready, eager, and powerful to save.

The four men overcame all difficulties. They found the house crowded where Jesus was preaching and teaching. So they made a hole in the roof of the house just over the place where Jesus was, and let the man down on his bed before Jesus. They waited and, no doubt, prayed that Jesus would do something for the man. He did! When he saw *their* faith, he forgave the man's sins, healed his body, and sent him on his way rejoicing.

Adults can be brought to Jesus. Jesus will save adults. Your group can bring men or women, one by one, to Jesus. These four men brought this man on his bed and Jesus saved him.

Are you willing to try it out? Good! Select, with your pastor, superintendent, and your teacher, a prospect who belongs to your group. Do not look for an easy one. Select a needy one. *Pray* earnestly. Let every member of the group, after earnest prayer, go to see the prospect. Go in the faith that Jesus wants you to go. Go believing that he will save the person in question.

Talk to the person in his home. Say and mean: "We will be in a car in front of your house next Sunday morning. We want you to go with us to Sunday school." If necessary and desirable, arrange for other workers to do the same thing for other members of the family.

Will the man respond? Certainly he will. Will such an effort cause excitement? Yes, it will. The people in the case recorded in the fifth chapter of Luke went home saying to one another, "We have seen strange things to day." The point is, the man was saved. It took extreme efforts to get him saved, but mark it down—he was saved.

Remember, Jesus did an extreme thing when he died on the cross. Are we willing to do whatever is necessary to get people to Jesus?

The teacher and president of a class will find in the group plan a very practical way for enlisting in personal soul-winning all the members of a Sunday school class.

The pastor, educational director, and general superintendent will find an enthusiastic response from Adults and Young People when they take time to train the group leaders and members.

The group plan is a church program of work with and through the Adults. It is sufficient and adequate for evangelism, enlargement, enlistment, and giving.

Here is a practical plan to provide Christian homes for more children. Here is a practical plan for making evangelists out of those evangelized. Some of the most effective, personal soul-winners in the churches are men and women won to the Lord and trained and immediately put to work in their classes and in other places.

Pastors will find success in winning adults when they take time to enlist and train and work with the group leaders in the Adult Sunday school classes.

The plan is not automatic. It calls for the leadership of pastor, superintendent, all department officers, and teachers. Using the group plan is simple and practical. It has permanency to it. It is not a question of finding time to direct this plan of work. Many churches have found it to be the best plan to produce the desired results in a church.

## V. Where Does Your Class Stand?

Here are reports from classes showing the results in winning people to Christ when there is room for growth in a class and when the class is small enough for teacher and class members to have a close personal relationship. Mr. Royce Bryant, superintendent of the Sunday school in Central Park Baptist Church, Birmingham, Alabama, gives four splendid testimonies:

"A class of men, Mr. J. Rex Brown, teacher, began the year October 1, 1952, with nine on the roll and had forty on the roll Promotion Day, 1953. During the year fourteen men from this class joined the church on profession of faith and nine by letter.

"Another class of men taught by Mr. C. B. Neugent began the year on October 1, 1952, with fourteen on the roll and closed the year with twenty-four on the roll. During this year seven men joined the church on profession of faith and five by letter.

"Another class of men taught by Dr. Cas Reagan began the year October 1, 1953, with an enrolment of nineteen and had thirty-six on the roll the first of

March, 1954. During this five-month period three men joined the church on profession of faith, and five joined by letter."

Continuing, Mr. Bryant reports:

"We have our Adults graded into nine departments and fifty-six classes. We observe annual promotion with our Adults. The teachers begin each year with a new class, and a class enrolment small enough for growth. In that way there is a strong incentive for a class to enrol lost people and win them to Christ. The attendance of our Sunday school has averaged 1,616 since October 1, 1953 through February, 1954. This is a net gain of 190 per Sunday over the same period one year ago."

How does your class measure up to the test of winning lost people? Is it closely graded? Is it small enough to encourage growth? Is it organized on the group plan? Is it assigned definite prospects? Is it working, visiting, praying regularly to enrol and win the lost?

### Questions for Review

1. What evidences can you cite to show that adults have been won for Christ?
2. Give four reasons why there are so many adults in our country today who are not enrolled in Sunday school.
3. How do you account for the success of churches in winning adults today?
4. Show how the group plan functions to increase the number of adults won by any Sunday school.

# 3. PARENTS MUST BE WON

A nineteen-year-old boy sat in a small cell in death row. "I never had a Christian home. My parents never went to Sunday school. I never heard my father or mother pray." Two fifteen-year-old girls were arrested at midnight on the streets of one of our cities. The mother of one of the girls was found in a beer joint. Ask the girls this question: "Did you ever go to Sunday school?" Their answer will be, "No, we never went, because our mothers never took us." Such statements justify the use of the word "must" in the title of this chapter.

Surely the word "must" is not too strong. Parents must be won. It is difficult, often impossible, to win the children when the parents are wrong. The first immediate obligation, certainly one of the most pressing obligations, is to win the parents. There are many important reasons why parents must be won to the Lord Jesus Christ.

## I. For the Sake of Assuring Christian Parenthood

Let us consider the figures studied in chapter 1. There are 11,500,000 babies under four years of age now living in these United States, and four out of five of these babies are not enrolled in any Sunday school.

Who are the parents of these babies? Many of them are not Christians. Others are church members who have grown indifferent. They do not attend any church services. In many cases the parents belong to different denominations. In other cases one parent is a Christian, and the other is not. Some of the parents of these babies are members of churches where no provision has been made for married Young People or younger Adults. Strange to say, some churches do not even yet have a Cradle Roll department to minister in the homes, nor any Nursery provisions for the babies on Sunday morning to make it easy for parents to attend the Sunday school.

Every child deserves a Christian home. The solemn truth is that many children will never have a Christian home unless your church and my church shall win the parents to Christ, church membership, and Christian living. The fact may be startling, but it is true. This fact gives all the reasons any church needs for departments and classes for married Young People and also for younger Adults.

It is usually very difficult to win children to Christ when the parents are not Christians.

In a recent experience of a pastor and church, efforts were made to win three children whose parents were not Christians. These parents were good, moral, successful people, but they were not Christians. The children were all in the teen-age years. While year by year the parents waited and delayed making a decision for Christ, one of the girls died. Even then the parents refused to take Christ as their Saviour. The remaining two children likewise refused to accept Christ, even though they readily acknowledged their need of a Saviour.

Finally, one Sunday morning in the church service, the parents walked down the aisle together and said publicly, "We take Jesus as our Saviour." Immediately, from different sections of the church building, came the son and daughter. When the parents made their surrender, the children followed. Of course, our hearts go out even now to the other girl who died without Christ.

Why did the parents linger? Surely they were accountable for their negligence. But had the church done all that was possible to win these parents while the children were small? When this couple married, did the church have a department and classes for the married Young People? Churches have a tremendous accountability in their efforts to win lost people.

## II. For the Sake of the Children

Most Southern Baptist Sunday school workers know Mr. and Mrs. Sibley C. Burnett. They have two lovely children. While these children were of Primary age, they both trusted Jesus voluntarily and joined the church where their parents belonged. Now they are older and several years away from that vital, supremely important decision. Sibley Charles and Mary Roanna are both active, happy, radiant Christians. You will find them in their places regularly in the worship services, prayer meeting, Sunday school, Training Union, Vacation Bible school, and all special church activities where children and young people are expected to participate. They exert a beautiful, uplifting influence in school, at home, at play, and in all places where young people go. Here we see the results of Christian parents.

A superintendent reports: "We have more than 100 Juniors enrolled in our Sunday school. All except three of our Juniors whose parents are in Sunday school and who attend the preaching services regularly are already Christians. It is easy to win boys and girls to Christ where the parents are active Christians."

A letter from a superintendent states that of 47 Junior boys and girls in his Sunday school who are not Christians, 43 of them are from homes where the parents are not Christians, or where the parents do not attend Sunday school, or where the parents are not together in a church. In some cases a mother is a member of the church, and the father is not. In other cases one parent belongs to one denomination, and the other is a member of another denomination. Continuing, the superintendent states that it is easy to win boys and girls when both parents are together and active in attendance and service in the church.

Winning parents to Christ and helping them have Christian homes is close to the heart of the work of a church.

### III. For the Sake of Moral Standards

Wherever the Bible has gone, there have been better moral standards and higher levels of living conditions. The Bible, when taught and practiced, always changes moral and living conditions upward.

The Sunday school is the friend of the home. It trains children to be kind and courteous. It teaches children to be truthful and honest. It guides youth in making right choices. The Sunday school provides a place where men and women meet and associate with the best people. In the Sunday school you make friends who live on a high moral plane, friends who make it easier for those who are weak to live happy, useful lives.

The Sunday school gives people of all ages a Christian philosophy of life. People who attend Sunday school regularly receive deposits in their lives out of which strong moral character is made. Bible study gives assurance that it is profitable to live a clean life, and useful life. The influence of the Sunday school is a strong bulwark of moral strength for people of all ages.

It is most unusual to find before the courts a boy or

girl, man or woman, who has attended Sunday school regularly from early childhood. It is even more unusual to find young people before the courts when both parents attend the church services regularly and practice daily Bible reading in the home.

In Mississippi a Sunday school was organized in a community where moral conditions were low. In less than five years there was a decided change for the better in the moral conditions in that community. Today, after ten years, the moral conditions are even higher. No longer are the officers of the law forced to visit this community except to protect the children as they cross the streets on their way to school or to assist with the traffic of the churchgoers on Sunday.

Place enough Sunday schools in all the communities of the world to provide for all the people. Staff these Sunday schools with plain, Christian men and women who love the Bible, live its teachings, and who love people, and soon the streams of healing will destroy selfishness, lust, and greed and surplant them with love, purity, and service.

The chief of police in a Mississippi city went to his pastor's study one day to tell him that the Bible-teaching program of their church had done more to relieve the city of juvenile and adult delinquency than his police force could ever do.

## IV. For the Sake of the Future

Parents must be won for the sake of the future. Again, let us consider the eleven and a half million babies under four years of age now living in these United States. If you recall, only one out of five of these children are enrolled in Sunday school. Will you move out decade by decade and imagine conditions with this four-year age span of life if these children are not provided with Christian parents and Christian homes and won to Christ now?

If, when the children now under four come to the high-school years, and four out of five of them are not Christians, what will be the condition in the public schools? If four out of five of them are not Christians during the period when they are in the later teen-age years, what of the moral standards? When these more than eleven million individuals become of voting age, if four out of five of them are not Christians, what will be the decisions on election day?

Mother, your little girl now under four years of age will likely marry some time. If she reaches that period in her life, and four out of five of her friends are not Christians, the chances are that she will marry a man who is not a Christian, and the odds will be against the children having a happy, Christian home. If four out of five of the little children now living are not led to become Christians, what effect will it have in the churches in the years that are ahead? When death comes sometime out there, and four out of five are not Christians, will the eternal record of the churches of today be free from the blood of the neglected?

Does all this seem fantastical, unreal, and extreme? Did you know that our boasted and cherished Christian civilization is just one generation from paganism? Listen to and ponder well what happened in the days of Joshua:

"And the people served the Lord all the days of Joshua, and all the days of the elders that outlived Joshua, who had seen all the great works of the Lord, that he did for Israel. And Joshua the son of Nun, the servant of the Lord, died, being an hundred and ten years old. . . . And also all that generation were gathered unto their fathers: and there arose another generation after them, which knew not the Lord, nor yet the works which he had done for Israel. And the children of Israel did evil in the sight of the Lord, and served Baalim: and they forsook the Lord God of their fathers, which brought them out of the land of Egypt, and followed other gods, of the gods of the people that were round about them, and bowed themselves unto them, and provoked the Lord to anger. And they forsook the Lord, and served Baal and Ashtaroth. And the anger of the Lord was hot against Israel, and he delivered them into the hands of spoilers that spoiled them, and he sold them into the hands of their enemies round about, so that they could not any longer stand before their enemies. Whithersoever they went out, the hand of the Lord was against them for evil, as the Lord had said, and as the Lord had sworn unto them: and they were greatly distressed" (Judg. 2:7-8, 10-15).

The people who forsook the Lord and served Baal and Ashtaroth were only one generation removed from the influence of Joshua and the godly elders. What will happen in any society which, for just one generation, neglects to win the parents and make Christ central in the homes? Our $17,000,000,000 crime bill of today is at least partially the result of the neglect of the churches of yesterday. Are the churches today doing better in winning parents and boys and girls?

### V. Many Churches Are Winning Parents

This testimony from Mrs. E. Gregson Brown, associate superintendent of the married Young People's department, First Baptist Church, Jacksonville, Florida, is typical of classes and departments that are now ministering to married Young People in an increasing number of churches.

"Our married Young People have an important

place in the life of our church. Every few weeks a new baby comes into one of their homes, and we try to see that he or she is enrolled as soon as possible, in the Cradle Roll department. Before long, the baby becomes a member of the Nursery department. It has been our joy as leaders to see many young wives and husbands come to Christ. We have learned from experience that many of these young couples are away from home for the first time and that their need for Christian friends and the influence of a spiritual church is very vital.

"Building Christian homes is the business of this department, and accepting Christ as Saviour is the beginning of a Christian home. We feel also great pride and satisfaction in seeing our young people serving in other departments of the Sunday school and active in all phases of the church program.

"We were assigned a goal of 15 net enrolment gain for the year. Our present enrolment is 84, a net gain of 15 in five months. We reached our goal during the first few months. We are not going to be satisfied and take it easy, for we have agreed that we will start all over and enrol 15 more members for our department, our church, and our Lord. The more we reach for Sunday school, the more we will win for Christ."

There are married young women in your community waiting for a teacher just like Mrs. Guy Jones, of First Baptist Church, Jacksonville, Florida—a teacher to help them. Hear the testimony of Mrs. Jones:

"Working with Young People for the past twenty years has been one of the greatest joys of my Christian experience.

"At present my class consists of fifteen married girls from seventeen to twenty years of age. Our first purpose is to enrol them in the Sunday school, one of the greatest agencies of our church for winning to Christ those who are lost. As they read God's Word in the class, listen to the truth explained, hear the testimony of other young wives and mothers, and participate in the lesson discussion, their hearts are made ready for the work of the Holy Spirit. Then, when a Christian friendliness is shown and they are invited to sit with the teacher or some member of the class at the worship service, quite often on the first or second Sunday they respond to the invitation by accepting Christ and confessing him before men. During my years of teaching I have seen many of my pupils take this step, and the thrill never lessens.

"To see one's pupils grow in Christian grace and become leaders in winning others is the greatest reward any teacher could desire."

Is it too much to say that the smallest church should have two classes for married Young People, one for men and one for women? Someone says: "In our community there are no more than five couples twenty-four years of age and under; therefore, we cannot have the two classes."

Let's face the need. The fact remains that such a church in the small community does need two classes, one for the five men and one for the five women. These five couples need Christ, the church, the influence of Christian people. They need help in their Christian lives. They need encouragement as they seek to rear their children. Experience in many churches shows that even when the numbers are limited, these married Young People will come much nearer getting the help they need in the two separate classes than they will in any other known way. Separate classes for men and women enable each group to come close to a sympathetic teacher and to each other. Each class will be limited to persons in the 17-24 age range.

Then, certainly the younger Adults need classes for men and classes for women. If the church membership is small and the prospects are limited, one class for each sex, twenty-five through thirty years of age, may be all that will be needed. Let the number of classes be determined by the needs and not by the condition of the building, nor by the imaginary idea that teachers are not available, nor by the present enrolment of people of any particular age span.

Your church can win the parents if you will face the need and then supply whatever it takes to meet the need. Pray and work until the teachers have been enlisted. Provide a meeting place even if such meeting place has to be outside the church building. Go out and lovingly invite the people to come, and they will respond. Your church can win the parents.

### VI. An Aim, an Invitation, and a Plan

Southern Baptist Sunday schools have a worthy aim. It is: "A Christian Home for Every Child." You cannot by-pass the churches and build Christian homes. The aim is "A Christian Home for Every Child," but you start with the church to provide that home. Jesus gave to his church the task of winning people to Christ. The Christian homes of today are the fruits of the work of the churches.

There are not many Christian homes in communities where there are no churches. You can help provide Christian homes for more and more children by enlisting the unsaved parents in Sunday school, Training Union, and all regular church services. You can train every mature Christian man and woman to be regular and faithful in the preaching services of the church and the prayer meetings by training them in the Sunday school and Training Union.

A church, through the Sunday school and Training Union, can place in the hands of parents Christian literature, which always has an uplifting influence and guides people along right ways.

Homes that are not Christian will not seek or even request Christian literature. Churches must take the initiative.

A church, through the Sunday school and Training Union, can lead parents to study regularly the Bible and the important business of Christian living. A church, through the use of the Sunday school and Training Union, can put parents in the preaching services. Through these means a church can train and enlist in service parents of all ages. A church, through the Sunday school and Training Union, can encourage and strengthen parents in daily Christian living. A church, through the Sunday school and Training Union, has a most effective means of helping parents establish family altars.

The invitation is: "Take Your Family to Sunday School." The invitation to attend Sunday school is attractive. It is an invitation that all Christian Sunday school members can give. "Come with your family and study the Bible with us," can be extended to multitudes of people not now in Sunday school by the multitudes of people who are in Sunday school.

The invitation "Take Your Family to Sunday School" involves Bible study and preaching attendance. It provides the best possible evangelistic approach. It leads to membership and participation in the Training Union. It provides regular givers through church programs on stewardship of money. It is often the beginning of a Christian home. It is the first step in the development of Christian character.

The plan, "Provide in Every Church for Every

Member of Every Family," is a call to every church to make balanced provision in the Sunday school for all age groups. The aim and the invitation will be largely fruitless unless the plan is carried out with understanding.

The continued practice of the aim, invitation, and plan by all Baptist Sunday schools is the direct way to change our ratio of baptisms to church members from one to twenty to one to eight. It is the way to success in the things the Bible outlines for churches to do.

Parents must be won, and churches by the use of the Sunday school can win them. Win the parents and you win the children. Win both parents and children, and the future is secure.

### Questions for Review

1. Give four compelling reasons why parents must be won.
2. As you read the testimonies of churches which have baptized numbers of parents during recent years, list the provisions which have been most fruitful for winning parents.
3. State the aim, the invitation, and the plan which outline the direct way to change the ratio of baptisms in Southern Baptist churches from one to twenty to one to eight.

# 4. YOUNG PEOPLE CAN WIN YOUNG PEOPLE

It is a beautiful sight to see two young people walk down the aisle of a church building in response to the invitation in the regular preaching services, one of them a Christian coming with a friend he has led to Christ during the week. Can this be made a regular occurrence in all the churches? The evidence shows that it is possible.

Young people admire young people. Young people influence young people. They are loyal to each other. They work tirelessly and enthusiastically in any cause they love, provided they have responsibilities in it. They are capable and can do effective work. Because of these and other characteristics, young people can win young people.

Let's call some pastors and others to the witness stand for testimonies.

## I. Young People Are Winning Young People

We call Harold D. Tallant, pastor of the First Baptist Church, Madisonville, Kentucky, for a testimony:

"The number of Young People in our Sunday school increased from 12 to 171 in a period of five years. During the five years I baptized 22 single Young People and 98 married Young People and received by letter 30 single Young People and 87 married Young People. My experience compels me to know that young people can be won and that young people can and will help win young people.

"When our Young People's department was first organized in 1948, there were 12 Young People in two classes. With a lot of praying and hard work, the enrolment of the Young People increased steadily. By 1951 there were 171 enrolled in ten classes. By this time we had two departments for Young People—one for the married and one for the single.

"Our Young People, through the period of planning and building, were willing to occupy crude, temporary quarters in order that we might have two great departments. In our new church they have a lovely assembly room, all their own, and six classrooms. Our married Young People also have a new department assembly room and five classrooms.

"The plans that were laid, the new departments and classes that were organized a few years ago, now are paying off. Since the organization of our Young People into departments, we have been able to minister to the multitude of Young People. As a pastor I hold the interests of the young people close to my heart. I realize that the future success of any church lies in the utilization of its young people.

"In a recent revival in our church many of our young fathers came to know Jesus as personal Saviour. Perhaps they would not have been reached, especially at this particular time, had not provision been made for them in the Sunday school. Many of our young people have already dedicated their lives to specific full-time Christian service, while a host of others have said with Isaiah, 'Here am I; send me' to whatever field of service in whatever vocation God can use my life."

Here is a testimony from John Glenn, now student at Southwestern Seminary, regarding his experiences while he was a member of the First Baptist Church of Charlotte, North Carolina. Mr. Glenn was a young man winning young men.

"The greatest joy for a Sunday school teacher is to see the unsaved members of his class accept Christ as

Saviour. I recall one young man who visited the class I was teaching, enrolled, and, at the insistence of his girl friend, attended our Youth Retreat. While there, I had the opportunity in our cabin alone with him one afternoon to witness to him. He came under conviction and gave his heart to Christ a few months later.

"There are those who casually visit, such as the soldier who came to my Sunday school class. I took opportunity of visiting with him that Sunday afternoon, explaining to him the plan of salvation. That night he returned, and it was a thrill to see him step out and accept Christ as Saviour.

"There was the Catholic boy, who was sick of the formalities and rituals of religion. He was deep in sin, not only a breaker of the moral law, but condemned by society and contemplating suicide. What a joy it was, after days of entreaty and exhortation, to hear him tell me, 'I know now what it means to be born again,' as he accepted the Lord Jesus.

"Sometimes it takes longer, for patience must be a virtue of the teacher. There was the high-school graduate who realized his lost condition, yet 'would not give up good times,' as he expressed it, to accept Christ. Four years later the seed, which had earlier been sown, bore fruit as he publicly accepted Christ as his Saviour.

"Such activity on my part in working with young men in my class created in me the deep desire to serve my Lord, and I came under the conviction that he was calling me to full-time service. I have surrendered to his call and am now in Southwestern Seminary preparing myself for a larger and greater service. Now I know what it means to be in the center of God's will."

Here is a marvelous and encouraging testimony of successful work with and by young people. It is related by Miss Frances Hendrix, youth director of the

First Baptist Church, Jacksonville, Florida. Dr. Homer G. Lindsay is pastor and has led and supported the workers and young people in all this fine work.

"First Baptist Church, Jacksonville, Florida, is vitally interested in the salvation of the youth of this city and their spiritual growth toward Christian maturity.

"In September, 1949, there was one Young People's department in the Sunday school, with a total enrolment of 167. A little more than four years later, there are three Young People's departments with a total enrolment of 300.

"In October, 1949, the married Young People's department was created with an enrolment of 44. This department has experienced a gradual growth to a present enrolment of 84.

"Even though lack of space made it necessary to use an Adult classroom for the opening assembly, in October, 1953, we organized a new department for seventeen-year-olds (four classes). Beginning with an enrolment of 38, they have gained 8 new members in five months. Each unsaved pupil in this group has already been led to Christ and to church membership through the influence of the Sunday school. It is an evident fact that we are holding and ministering to the seventeen-year-old group much better than ever before.

"The incredible turnover in the single Young People's department (18-24 years) accounts for a ministry to at least twice the enrolment, which at present is 173. It is a significant fact that of all the hundreds of Young People who pass through our Sunday school, it is a very rare thing for one to leave without being won to Christ and church membership. We thank God for the opportunity of helping them.

"A fourth Young People's department is now being

organized to begin functioning when we enter our new building in a few months. We will then have Young People's departments for married young people, single 17-year-olds, single 18-20-year-olds, and single 21-24-year-olds. This means a growth of from *one* to *four* departments in a little more than four years.

"Look further with us! During the past year 50 per cent of all the additions to our church were Young People! *Fifty per cent* of all those baptized into our church were Young People! By Young People we mean those between the ages of 17-24. *Eighty-one* per cent of our Young People enrolled in Sunday school are tithers! Forty Young People are serving in places of leadership in other departments of the Sunday school. In a recent church-sponsored soul-winning training school there were 76 enrolled in the Young People's class. Within the past year 15 Young People have surrendered for full-time Christian service, and scores have rededicated their lives to Christ. What is responsible for all this?

"The blessings of the Lord and his gracious answering of our prayers are the fundamental causes.

"Our youth program encourages the co-operation and participation of the Young People in the entire program of the church.

"Our pastor is interested in his young people and in his Sunday school.

"We provide consecrated and stable adult leadership, carefully selected for work with Young People.

"We maintain a definite program of regular visitation by classes and departments.

"There is continual emphasis on evangelism from the pulpit, in the departments, and in the classes. The young people themselves do as much of the actual soul-winning among other young people in the Sunday school as the teachers and officers do. Isn't that as it should be?

"We magnify the Bible and its study on Sunday morning and on Wednesday night (teachers' meeting), and make concerted attempt to apply its teachings to the lives of young people.

"We have set the Standard of Excellence as a goal.

"We provide a well-planned program of wholesome social life and Christian fellowship."

How can the Sunday school be used to help young people win young people?

## II. Providing the Atmosphere and Opportunity for Soul-winning Among Young People

A church determines the response of young people. A positive, sympathetic attitude in a church toward young people, coupled with the best possible provision, always brings a happy response.

### 1. *The Atmosphere in a Church Is Vital*

"The young people in that church are wonderful," was a remark by one church member to another after a visit in the church involved. "They are wonderful," replied the friend. "Why are young people so different? They are not like that in our church."

The difference in the two churches was not in the young people, but in the atmosphere that prevailed in these churches. In the first church the young people had a feeling of belonging. In the second church the young people knew there were questions and unfavorable conversations about them.

### 2. *Recognition of Young People Is Essential*

One church in Atlanta, Georgia, has one young person, frequently two young persons, to make statements during the evening preaching hour. Sometimes the statement is an announcement, again a testimony, and at other times a brief message requiring not more than three or four minutes.

A church in Chattanooga, Tennessee, has three brief testimonies each Sunday evening as a part of the regular Sunday evening service. In the period of a year, 150 people have been recognized. Others are used during the prayer meeting hours.

In many churches the young people are used in the musical program. Young people like to sing, and they sing well. They will work hard in the preparation of special numbers. They can be used to sing, not in order to entertain or to be placed on exhibition, but as a vital part of the worship and work of a church.

### 3. *Provision for Young People Is Important*

There should be at least as many classrooms for Young People as for Juniors. The Junior age span includes four years, whereas the Young People's age span covers eight years.

The average class enrolment for Juniors is about 9.5, while the average class enrolment for Young People is 13. Quite often a church has eight classrooms for Juniors and only two for the Young People. This fact, more than any others, reveals why we have failed to enrol and hold our young people.

It is difficult for even adult men and women to see the logic in providing departments and classrooms in a building for people who are not even in attendance. It is true, however, that the provision in the building and the officers and teachers come before the enrolment of the class members. There is usually growth in any department when additional provisions are made for the growth.

John F. Havlik, pastor of the Beaumont Baptist Church, Kansas City, Missouri, gives this testimony:

"Eight years ago, this church decided to expand the organization enough to reach every possibility in the community. This provision, however, was limited to the elementary departments. What this church planned to do eight years ago is now a fact. In a recent census very few prospects could be found for the elementary ages. However, more than one thousand Young People and Adult prospects were found."

It is evident that the people in this church, just like the people in most churches, found difficulty in providing in the building and also in the organization for any age group that did not already have a good percentage of the age group enrolled.

When churches provide for Young People on the same equality as they have provided for Juniors, in a few years the majority of the Young People will be enrolled. A fuller study of this subject is presented in the last part of this chapter.

There has developed through the years a false conception, promoted by a few and accepted by many, that young people are "different," and that young people will not attend church services. Are young people essentially "different"? Most of the characteristics of youth are commendable. When young people are "bad," the cause can usually be traced to adults.

Often the generally accepted moral standards in a community, or the attitudes and practices of adults, have a strong influence upon the actions and attitudes of young people. One place that sells whiskey, beer, and the like, and encourages the "gang" to "hang around," can, in a generation, color the moral attitudes of young people, unless in the community there is a stronger influence for good that touches their lives.

### III. Training Young People to Be Effective Soul-winners

The young people will do today and tomorrow what the churches train them to do.

Training young people in evangelism will prove to be profitable to a pastor and a church. It will certainly be profitable to the young people. Young people need two types of training for soul-winning: one, a study of the Bible teachings about the plan of salvation; and the other, practical experience in dealing with lost people.

A week of preparation led by the pastor will bring pastor and young people close together in a helpful, holy fellowship that will greatly expand the work of the pastor. There are many good books available. *Soul-Winning Doctrines* by J. Clyde Turner is a most helpful book. *Every Christian's Job* by C. E. Matthews is an excellent study.

It will be essential for the pastor to select several Scripture passages and guide the young people in a study of these passages and in a discussion of how to use them in dealing with lost people. As the study proceeds, let the pastor visit with one or two of the young people until they can throw off the spirit of timidity and begin to learn how to approach people and deal with people.

Let visitation by the pastor, with one or two selected young people, continue long after the week of training, until all the young people have received this practical help. Let this be only the beginning of the training of young people in the important task of winning other young people to Christ. Young people will develop a concern for the salvation of other young people as they are led to win people to Christ.

## IV. Using Young People in the Class Organization

The group plan of class organization has practical and unlimited possibilities for good in the utilization of young people. The plan is the division of a class into groups of about four class members, with one of the members as the leader of the group. To begin with, the members of the group will likely be Christians and members of the church.

Each group should be assigned prospective members. The actual work is done in the following way: The pastor, general superintendent, department superintendent, and teacher will see that each group has regularly one or two prospects. The group leader will use the Christian members of his group to enlist the prospects. As soon as one prospect has been enrolled, the group leader should be assigned another. The prospects will be enrolled through visitation.

Young people like to work together. The leaders in a Sunday school can encourage the group to visit together. Let the four or five members of a group go together in one car to visit a prospect. It works like this: If there are three groups in the class, and four classes in the department, then there are twelve groups. The visitation day is Thursday, and the hours for the Young People's departments are 7: 00 to 9: 00 o'clock in the evening. The four classes, including their teachers, meet at the church building at 7: 00 o'clock. In churches in villages and open country, the time may be Sunday afternoon or Saturday evening.

Under the guidance of the superintendent or associate superintendent there is a period of prayer and brief reports of various activities of the classes. If there is no department organization, then this guidance will be under the direction of the teacher and president of each class. By 7:20 o'clock the groups are off for one hour and twenty minutes of visitation. There are as many cars as there are groups. Each group goes after *one* prospect.

The teacher may go with groups occasionally, but not always. If he does, the group members will let the teacher do the work, and they will soon lose interest.

After the group has seen the prospect, there will be time to visit any sick member of the group or an absentee. Really, the group should go by the home of an absentee on the way to see the prospect and take the member who was absent the previous Sunday along to visit the prospect. This is important.

When a group grows to six or eight in number, it should be given recognition for work well done, and two groups should be started from the one. When two, three, or four new groups have been organized, and the groups average four to five per group, a new class should be organized. This is the way of growth, and growth of the Sunday school is the sure way, the permanent way to bring people to Christ.

The teacher should visit every week. The teacher will set the example for all the groups. There are many, many reasons why the teacher should visit. There are lost members of the class to be won. There are sick members to be visited. There are individuals with personal problems. There are assignments of work to be made. There are group leaders to be trained and encouraged. There are important matters that the teacher and class president must discuss.

The president should visit. The president may visit with the respective groups. There may be cases that will require the personal attention of the president.

Every member of every class can be led to have a vital part in the soul-winning work of a church. Use all the class members to visit the prospects, and soon there will be developed a spirit of victory, expectancy, and interest that happily impels young people on in their quest for other young people.

If the groups and classes are allowed to grow too large, the members of the group will find themselves visiting the absentee members of the class, rather than leading every member of the class to visit and help win new people. Keep the groups small in number and keep the groups visiting prospects, and you can enlist all the young people, and at the same time keep enrolling and winning new people.

## V. Developing Young People Through Guided Responsibility

The Training Union has let us see just how effective young people are, and how eager they become when the work of a church is turned over to them during Youth Week.

Many of the young people are in the Training Union doing their best to learn how to become effective, fruitful workers in the church and community. A Sunday school class organized into groups of four or five members is an ideal place and way for these young people to put into practice what they are learning in the Training Union. You see, the two lines of work with young people are needed—both are essential.

Look for a moment at these two important phases of the work with young people. One, of course, is to get the vital work of a church accomplished. Another is to develop all the young people so that now and later all of them will be capable workers for the Lord. Always the temptation is to use the most apt individuals to do all the work. Is this fair to the more timid ones or to the more reserved ones? Often the reserved or timid individual has hidden powers that will, when called out and used, far exceed those of the more forward individual.

Would it be profitable to work on the basis that every young person can be enlisted? Let the churches work earnestly to enlist, train, and use all the young people, and in a few decades our churches will be filled with interested members who are capable in many phases of the work of the Lord.

Young people like responsibility. They grow under responsibility. They develop a love for their church when they are given responsibility.

Thousands and thousands of fine young people have had desires stifled and willingness dampened. This has been done by teachers who lecture to those present and criticize the young people who are not present, yet who do very little to encourage, plan, and direct the activities that would use and develop young people.

A pastor and superintendent gave a young man responsibilities. He felt that others could do the tasks better than he, but because of the recognition and request of his pastor and superintendent, he did his best. He grew and developed under responsibility. Today he is a useful man largely because of the recognition and assignments made by those who loved him and took time to help him grow.

## VI. Securing Understanding Teachers

Undoubtedly, the greatest factor in guaranteeing reaching, teaching, winning, and developing young people is the right kind of teachers and workers for young people.

This testimony from Mrs. H. E. Barnett, secured by Mr. O. D. Horton, shows the worth of a real teacher. Says Mr. Horton:

"I had heard often of the wonderful record of Mrs. H. E. Barnett as a teacher of seventeen-year-old girls in First Baptist Church, San Antonio, Texas. I wanted to know how she had succeeded in doubling her class in the first quarter after promotion and how she trippled it before the end of the year. Here is her answer:"

> I have taught for thirty years. Each week I contact every member of my class. In that way I can know all the members of the families and the conditions in the homes. I come to know the mothers, the fathers, the grandmas, the old maid aunts, and even the maids.
>
> This is the one reason that my class has never failed in thirty years to reach the quota given by the superintendent. That is the reason the class doubled its enrolment in the first quarter and trippled it during the year.
>
> It is not too easy to build a class in our church. My class is made up of girls from all over San Antonio, and all the five high schools are represented. But the emphasis of the class (John 15:12) does away with all cliques and all sorority and school unfriendliness.
>
> We try to make the social hungers of the girls contribute to their spiritual growth. I take the girls to a camp house in June each year. We have a common purse, and two girls are given the purse and serve as hostesses for a day. They plan the meals and buy the food, and all share in the duties of the house.
>
> We have Scripture reading morning and evening and prayer in connection with each meal. At our last camp two girls were converted. They

and others spent much of the night in prayer, conversation, and rejoicing.

I have found that a Christian girl wants to be true. But I know that she will surely be tried. She likes to be trusted and will strive to be worthy of the trust of someone. I like to encourage my girls to trust the Lord and to love the Lord's people by showing them that I trust them.

I have been richly repaid for my thirty years' work with girls. A partial check on girls who have been in my class reveals that fourteen of the presidents have been listed in *Who's Who in Colleges and Universities.* Twelve are public schoolteachers, fourteen have graduated from Baylor, and three from Mary Hardin-Baylor. Eight have married preachers, and one is an educational director. To my knowledge, eighty-five girls from my class have attended Baptist colleges, and forty-seven have gone to other colleges.

If I have ever helped just one girl in my thirty years of teaching, I shall be happy for all eternity.

The following testimony from the experiences of Miss Hazel Stubbs, First Baptist Church, Jacksonville, Florida, reveals the possibilities in thousands of churches:

"If any girl in my class is not a Christian, my primary aim is to win her to Christ as soon as possible. Once when I received a new class by promotion, there was one girl enrolled who was not a Christian. She had a wonderful personality, and the other girls loved her, but she did not possess Christ as Saviour.

"I visited this girl, carried her home many times after church services, often talking with her about her salvation, and prayed for her constantly. Other members of the class and department were also praying for her. Then one night, when the invitation was given, she surrendered and made a public profession of her faith.

"She became a changed individual and was immediately ready to go out and win others. We made visits together to see friends of hers who were lost. She has been influential in enlisting many of them in Sunday school and then in leading them to Christ and church membership. She has told me how happy she is and how happy her mother was made by her decision. She said that she had never really felt the need of becoming a Christian until someone had seemed concerned about her. Are there others like her? Yes, multitudes!"

## VII. Planning to Enrol More Young People

Since results in thousands of churches reveal that increased Sunday school enrolment means an increased number of baptisms, it seems churches are not only justified but obligated to do everything possible to keep on increasing the Sunday school enrolment. This is as true with Young People as it is with Juniors.

What have been the steps followed by churches that have had a measure of success in enrolling young people in Sunday school? A study of the means used by successful churches shows that the methods are similar. Certainly, back of these means you find the spirit, concern, attitude, and the never-lifting compassion of the pastors, superintendents, department superintendents, and teachers of the Young People. Here are the essential steps used in reaching young people:

1. Provide departments and classes for the seventeen- and eighteen-year age span. In smaller churches one department and two or more classes may suffice. In larger churches there should be one or more de-

partments for the seventeenth year, and a department for the eighteenth year, with needed classes for girls and needed classes for boys in each department.

2. Provide departments and classes for nineteen- through twenty-four-year-old single Young People. In smaller churches provide one department with a minimum of two classes; in larger churches a department for ages nineteen through twenty years, and a second department for ages twenty-one through twenty-four years, with the needed number of classes for men and women in each department.

3. Provide a department for all married Young People under twenty-five years of age, with a class or classes for women, and a class or classes for men. Even the smallest church will need a department and two classes. Larger churches will need two or more departments and four or more classes in each department.

4. In college-centered churches, set up a department and classes for nonresident students, ages seventeen through twenty-four, where the number justifies. In some few churches two or more departments will be needed. Since training for service is a major purpose in any school, the department and classes for nonresident students should be graded, organized, and conducted on the same basis as Baptist churches generally use. When this plan is followed in school situations, young people return home with the "know how," and also the experience immediately to take their places of leadership in the churches to which they go.

5. Make provision for young people in uniform. Any complete plan of providing for young people must include those seventeen through twenty-four who have entered, or will enter, military service. For as long as anyone can foresee, our young men will have to

spend a period of their lives away from home in the armed forces. Many young women are serving, too.

The Military Service Membership Plan provides for a regular Sunday school ministry by the home church to absent servicemen and women of Young People's ages, seventeen through twenty-four.

Young People's classes and departments carry on the ministry by mailing the Young People's lesson quarterly each quarter, sending the church bulletin, writing personal letters, etc.

Through the use of this plan a young person away in the armed forces may continue to be counted as enrolled in his home Sunday school in the same manner that members of the Cradle Roll and Extension departments are counted.

By thus keeping strong the ties with its Young People in service, the home church can more easily re-enlist them as regular members of Sunday school promptly upon their return to civilian life.

Complete information on the Military Service Membership Plan may be obtained by ordering the free leaflet "A Positive Ministry to Servicemen and Women," from your state Sunday school secretary.

### Questions for Review

1. How does the experience of the First Baptist Church, Madisonville, Kentucky, demonstrate that Young People can be won?
2. Give three essentials for reaching Young People in any Sunday school.
3. Explain how the group plan of class organization functions to train and use Young People in soul-winning.
4. Give the steps to be followed by any church which desires to change the ratio of baptisms by enrolling more Young People in Sunday school.

# 5. SURE FOUNDATIONS FOR WINNING BOYS AND GIRLS

Dr. Hight C Moore once said, "It is easy for boys and girls to believe, but they must believe." Tests in many meetings of Christian workers show that nearly all our church leaders accepted Christ as Saviour early in life. These two facts give deep significance to the work of a church in winning boys and girls.

## I. The Winning of Boys and Girls Is Crucial in Christian Teaching

The majority of boys and girls of the age span nine through twelve years do accept Christ as Saviour and trust him for salvation when the following five conditions prevail: (1) when the child is brought to Sunday school early in life; (2) when both parents are Christians; (3) when both parents are regular in attendance in Sunday school, the preaching services, and Training Union; (4) when family prayers and Bible study in the home are observed; (5) when a church provides good teachers for the boys and girls.

These things do not—cannot—save. It is Jesus who does the saving. God's primary dealings are with the individual. Men and means may point the way, but they are no part of the way. There comes a time and a point where the individual must go alone with God through Christ and make his own decision and place personal faith in Jesus for salvation. That experience of stepping from the kingdom of Satan to the kingdom of God is a step with Christ alone.

The Sunday school workers and parents, however, have definite responsibilities. Paul said to Timothy, "From a child thou hast known . . ."

The teacher is God's husbandman. The teacher must prepare the ground, plant the good seed, water it, watch over it, keep the plant in contact with the right soil, and keep the surroundings as free as possible from things that would sap its vitality.

What is the means through which Jesus Christ reaches the soul and with which the teacher must keep the human soul in closest contact? It is the Bible, the record of God's revelation of himself to man, completed in Christ, the Word who became flesh and dwelt among men—full of grace and truth. Christ, the incarnate Word and the Bible, the revealed Word, are inseparably the Word of God.

Paul's charge to Timothy, "Preach the word," sums up the tasks of the churches today. Teach every individual we can reach to know the Word—Christ Jesus —the risen, living, reigning Lord; anchor every pulpit and every classroom to the proclamation of the Word.

The Bible must be the very basis of the Christian teacher's work. The Bible is not merely informational matter, but a living book. Other materials will be used, but only as illustration of biblical truth.

Getting the Word of God into the heart and life of man is the task of Christian education. It is not the skilful use of man-made techniques, but the effective workings of the Holy Spirit of God. In this the teacher is God's husbandman, nothing more, nothing less.

Here is the core of the whole question. Christian education must attempt no less and certainly no more than what the Bible teaches. This does not mean that the teacher is to sit back and wait for God to act. God has called his children into partnership with himself.

The teacher is, therefore, much more than just an educator, whose subject matter happens to be what is called *religion* rather than *science*. The teacher is a living instrument of the living God, a co-worker with him in the great task of bringing people under the power of the redeeming grace of God through the living Christ. This was Paul's conception of the work of the Christian teacher or preacher. "For we are labourers together with God" (1 Cor. 3:9).

The five things listed at the beginning of this chapter do lead boys and girls toward Jesus. These conditions prepare boys and girls for an early decision. Facts in thousands of cases support these statements. These are helpful surroundings that churches and homes can promote. Surely Jesus expects us to do all we can.

Not all boys and girls accept Jesus as Saviour during the age span of nine through twelve years. Often the home is a hindrance. It is difficult for a boy or girl to go over the wrong attitude or the indifference of a parent to get to Jesus. It is difficult for a Sunday school teacher to go over the wrong attitude of parents to bring boys and girls to Jesus. Right here is the binding obligation of a church to reach, win, and develop all such parents through the Adult provision in the Sunday school and Training Union.

Sometimes the church fails to provide the boys and girls with good teachers. Sometimes teachers are continued year after year even when they have gone an entire year without winning one person to Christ. Is this right? Is it fair to boys and girls who are lost to continue with an indifferent teacher, regardless of who he is or how attractive he may be? Usually the attitudes of teachers are changed when the attitude of the church is changed.

Some churches fail to provide in the church building for all the boys and girls. In many cases it would be impossible for even one half of the people in some communities to find standing room in the church building. When any church has eight classes for Juniors, four for Intermediates, and two for Young People, that church has definitely planned to lose one half of the Juniors in the Intermediate age span and three fourths of them during the Young People's age span.

The fact remains that boys and girls are susceptible to the gospel message. Many churches have found that the majority of boys and girls can be won to Christ when Christian influences are provided in the church and home.

## II. The Fruitfulness of the Foundation Ministry

Win a child and you help Jesus save a soul and a life. When a child is enrolled in the Cradle Roll, a church has made the first step toward winning that child's soul and life to Christ. This first step is not enough—it is only the *first* step. The child should be transferred to a Nursery department and brought to Sunday school every Sunday. This requires Nursery rooms, departments and classes for parents, and provisions to minister to the changing needs of the child as he grows.

Recently Mrs. H. R. Jones, superintendent of Nursery Sunday school work, was asked the question: "How many of the Nursery children who come up through the four years of the Nursery age span are lost from our rolls when they are promoted from the Nursery to the Beginner age span?" Mrs. Jones replied, "None of them, if anything like adequate provision has been made for the Beginner children." She is right. Children who are enrolled in a Nursery in Sunday school can easily be held in Sunday school through the Beginner, Primary, and Junior age spans.

What happens when adequate provisions are made and a boy or girl is held in Sunday school? In nearly every case the child accepts Christ as his Saviour during the Junior age span, sometimes in the last year of the Primary age span.

That is not all. The person who is won as a child develops into a faithful church member. That is not all. He comes to be a loyal, capable worker in the church. That is not all. He establishes and builds a Christian home. That is not all. He makes a good citizen and stands and works for the best things for a community, state, and nation. These areas of a life reveal something of the fruits reaped in a church through a Sunday school ministry that begins with the baby and continues through life.

What can a church do to guarantee that the children will be won to Christ?

## III. Favorable Conditions for Winning Boys and Girls

We have already seen in chapter 1 that there is a close relationship between the enrolment of a Sunday school and the rate of baptisms in the church. How can a church through its Sunday school make conditions favorable for winning boys and girls to Christ?

### 1. *Sunday School Attendance*

The very first step is enrolment in the Sunday school. Does it make any difference when boys and girls attend Sunday school from early childhood on? We will ask some churches to send representatives for testimonies.

Here is a testimony from Mrs. Keith C. Von Hagen, who has been superintendent of the Cradle Roll department in Belmont Heights Baptist Church, Nashville, Tennessee, for a period of years. This experience is one of many similar experiences coming as a result of the work of Mrs. Von Hagen and the Cradle Roll visitors who work so effectively with her.

"When they moved into our community, there were two little boys in the young couple's home. Mother was a Baptist but had not attended church services since childhood. Father was a Methodist. Very soon after their arrival in Nashville, the names of the two little boys were added to our Cradle Roll at Belmont Heights.

"It is not difficult to recall the visits made in the months that followed when the Cradle Roll visitor stood on the porch to talk to the mother, seldom to be invited inside.

"After five years a baby girl came into the home. She, too, became a member of the Cradle Roll department. This time it was easier to enrol her, for the mother seemed more appreciative of the ministry of the Sunday school. As the years passed, the boys came to Sunday school at irregular intervals, as a result of persistent and loving effort on the part of the age group leaders. They came to enjoy the experience more and more, however, and when they reached Junior ages, they could and did come to Sunday school by themselves. As a first- and a second-year Intermediate respectively, each boy surrendered his life to Christ.

"Little sister passed through the Cradle Roll and Nursery years without attending Sunday school and came only a few times during her Beginner years. Interest on the part of consecrated workers and her two big brothers is paying off now as she comes to the Primary department Sunday after Sunday. Along with her come her mother and daddy to take their places in Adult classes. Each member of the family is an active member of our church, except little sister, who, in her simple faith and earnest love, seems to be near to the kingdom of God.

"What if we who made the first contacts with the home had met their indifference with only halfhearted effort?"

Following is a testimony from the heart of Mrs. James W. White. Mrs. White has been superintendent of the Primary department in her church for nearly thirty years. It would be difficult to find a child who went all the way through her Primary department and did not accept Christ either in the last year of Primary age or during the Junior age span.

"During the years that I have served as superintendent of the Primary department, an average of thirty boys and girls have been promoted to the Junior department each year. This totals between 800 and 900 children.

"The greatest gift of all, and the one most wanted by Jesus, is the heart and life of a child. It is for this that we labor so lovingly and so patiently from year to year in the Primary department. Our great aim is to make wonderful truths given in the Bible become a part of the lives and characters of our Primary children.

"The boys and girls who attend Sunday school regularly while they are six, seven, and eight years of age, and who have Christian parents to encourage and aid them, almost without exception accept Christ as their Saviour during the years they are in the Junior department. In recent years a sizeable group each year has made decisions before graduating from the Primary department, though no pressure to this end has been made.

"Children from indifferent homes, who are permitted to miss Sunday school weeks or even months at a time, often pass through the golden years of opportunity without taking any stand for Christ. Years of living and waiting and praying and earnestly striving to win them are necessary.

"Much is to be gained, therefore, if we lend our very best efforts to enlisting and making regular attendance possible for little children and boys and girls in our Sunday school, keeping them under the influence of the precious Word of God."

2. *Growing Classes and Departments*

Keep departments and classes in growing condition as long as there are boys and girls not in Sunday school. A growing Sunday school provides a soul-winning opportunity in proportion to the growth of the Sunday school. As soon as a class of Juniors reaches eight or nine in enrolment, make two classes. Give each class one or two prospects at a time, and encourage the teachers and class members to enrol the prospects. Continue this expansion and assignment as long as there are boys and girls not enrolled in the Sunday school. The average attendance of a class of five is usually much better than a class of ten. Often the absentees are the unsaved members of a class. If a teacher has ten enrolled and five present, the temptation is to be satisfied. If the enrolment is six and the attendance is three, it is certainly more noticeable.

3. *New Sunday Schools*

In your immediate church community a census may not reveal more than six to ten Primaries, Juniors, or Intermediates not now in Sunday school. A careful survey of several other communities in the association may reveal that the majority of children and boys and girls out there are not in any Sunday school for the simple reason that these communities do not have Sunday schools. Many children and boys and girls are not in easy reach of a Baptist Sunday school. A good Sunday school placed in easy reach of people will immediately enlist some of them and, in a few months, many of them.

Workers with children and boys and girls should be actively engaged in seeing that a good Sunday school is provided within easy reach of every child and youth. When all the workers with children and boys and girls in a church combine to see that there is a Sunday school within easy reach of every person, they can lead a church to organize, one after another, the needed Sunday schools.

Since Sunday school enrolment and attendance provide maximum soul-winning opportunities for a church, then all Sunday school workers are obligated to see that every Sunday school continues to grow and that a Sunday school is provided in every community. This will be one of the most fruitful means of changing the ratio of baptisms to church members from one to twenty to one to eight.

4. *Christian Parents*

Because of the right of every boy and girl to have Christian parents, a church, through the Sunday school, is surely obligated to win parents to Christ for the sake of the children. That many boys and girls now enrolled in Sunday school have parents who are not Christians is cause sufficient to lead any class of men or women to examine their attitudes and their results in winning people. It is cause sufficient to win them to do anything and all that is needed to put the class in a position to win some boy's father or some girl's mother to Christ.

The adults in the Sunday school are as much obligated to win the parents of Juniors or Intermediates as are the officers and teachers of these boys and girls. When a class of men goes for five years and wins only two or three fathers to Christ, such a class becomes a stumbling block and needs to be replaced by small groups of men in classes of ten to twelve, where there is room to enrol and win lost men.

When a class of women with 500 or 50 enrolled goes for years without winning more than one mother a year, such class is in the way. It has missed the purpose of a Sunday school. It needs to be replaced by classes of eight to twelve women each with a leader, not a lecturer, who will make the winning of lost mothers the main job.

It is primarily a task for the church to see that the Sunday school functions in winning adults. This requires a church program, church provision, and a church spirit. A church can form a combination that makes it possible to win all the children. What is that combination? It is adequate provision in the Sunday school for every member of every family.

5. *Regular Bible Study*

Bible study is not only the heart of Sunday school work, it is the heart of winning people to Christ. Not only does the growth of the Sunday school increase the number of baptisms in a church, but where Bible study precedes the conversion experience, there is usually an early decision. When Bible study and Christian training follow the conversion experience, there is growth in the Christian life which soon results in Christian living and Christian service.

New Testament evangelism does not consist only in leading a person to make a profession of faith and be baptized. The new convert needs the food from the Word that will lead to full discipleship and Christian service.

## IV. More Teachers and Better Teachers Needed

The human tendency is for churches and leaders to depend upon a few, often one or two, faithful workers to enrol and minister to the children of any one of the age groups. No efforts are made to enlist and train other workers. When one of the faithful workers dies or moves, there is a hurried effort to get someone, often anyone, to take the place. This sounds like a dark picture, but in it we see a true picture. Sometimes the tendency is to imagine that the work in the Sunday school will be weakened when faithful workers relinquish the leadership or when classes are adjusted.

Until recently a mixed Adult class met in the auditorium. The age span of this class was from marriage to 50 plus. It was next to impossible to organize other classes. This class had not grown and had not won many people to Christ. Finally the church voted to grade the Adults and organize classes that had room for growth. In nine months' time this church baptized 70 Adults, and a report from the church states that more than 90 per cent of them came out of the Sunday school.

An oft repeated statement has been, "It is better to have a few good teachers than so many sorry ones." This false idea has been advanced in Sunday school work through the years. This attitude is deceptive and has led many churches in the wrong direction. Why should a church drift along on the false theory of "a few good workers"? Why not work on the basis of more good workers?

Churches that have drifted along on the theory that

a few good workers were better than so many poor ones have found one day that the so-called good ones were gone, and others had not been enlisted and trained to take their places.

Quite often one who passes as a good teacher is really scarcely more than an entertaining lecturer or one who can use words freely. Many times he is not a loyal church member. Usually this is not the fault of the teacher. He was asked by the class and may be doing the best he knows. The responsibility goes back to the church.

Usually when there is a teacher who fails to do good work and live a good life, it is due to neglect of the general officers and department workers.

When we read reports and see that 75 per cent to 85 per cent of all baptisms come from the Sunday school enrolment; when we hear judges of juvenile courts report that very few regular Sunday school attendants ever come into their courts; when we study the church treasurer's books and find that the people in Sunday school give about 88 per cent of all church offerings, even where one half of the church members are not in Sunday school; when we go in for the worship and preaching hour and see that 75 per cent to 85 per cent of those present came out of the Sunday school; when we consider these facts, we are bound to say that surely any church would profit by enlisting, training, encouraging, and using more and more Sunday school officers and teachers.

In fact, the vast majority of Sunday school workers are fine, faithful workers. They do win the lost, build up the Christians, strengthen the churches, help guarantee Christian homes, and develop Christian character in the lives of all who attend their departments and classes regularly. All churches need more good teachers for all ages. All churches can have more good officers and teachers.

### Questions for Review

1. State five conditions which, together, practically insure that a child will accept Christ as Saviour during the nine- to twelve-year age span.
2. What four major responsibilities rest upon a church for providing favorable conditions for winning boys and girls?
3. Why is providing for Adults such an important factor in winning boys and girls?

# 6. UNCHURCHED COMMUNITIES MUST BE OCCUPIED

"Is there anyone who cares enough to organize a church in our community where we can study the Bible and hear preaching?" It was the cry of a lost man in an unchurched community. It is the unspoken heart cry of tens of thousands of mothers and fathers who live out beyond the reach of our present churches. It is the unuttered cry of myriads of children without Christian parents. It is the sob of God over a lost community of men, women, boys, and girls. It is the cry every church must face and make a decision for or against.

The most fruitful field Southern Baptists have in the Convention territory for winning people to Christ is in branch stations or new work. There are three major reasons why this is true. First, new work usually grows much faster than the work in the older churches. Second, the percentage of lost people is far greater in the unchurched communities. Third, usually there are people in the unchurched communities who are waiting for the gospel message.

## I. There Are Multitudes of People Out Beyond the Practical Reach of the Present Churches

The majority of children and boys and girls not in Sunday school live beyond the easy reach of the present churches. In the territory where Southern Baptist churches are located, there are more than 20,000,000 people who live beyond the practical reach of the present churches. If these people are won to Christ, if these people have Bible study opportunities available, somebody must start churches in the communities where they live.

Cities are changing. The growth of most cities today is in the suburbs. Many communities spring up within a few months. Each of these communities needs one or more Baptist churches. The business concerns move with the people. Shops and stores are usually there in these communities when the people arrive. Why not the churches?

Dr. H. H. Hobbs, pastor of the First Baptist Church, Oklahoma City, Oklahoma, says:

"It has been estimated that American society is 61 per cent pagan. Every unchurched community is potentially a pagan cell in our nation. Only through the establishing of new Sunday schools or mission points can we hope to minister to the needs of the people in these communities.

"Every community will center upon some institution. If we do not furnish churches, then institutions of a destructive nature will fill the vacuum left by our indifference. Therefore it becomes our responsibility to see that a 'little colony of heaven' is established in every new community for the enlistment of the hearts and lives of the people in the cause of Christ."

## II. Every Church Needs a Department of Local Missions

Any church, regardless of the number of members, can begin a new work. Larger churches can support new work in several places. Discuss this question in prayer meeting in your church: Should our church desire to be the mother of another church? At another time discuss this question: Should our church have a department for local missions or for new work?

A church maintains a Junior department to enlist teachers and win the Juniors. Is it not just as essential for a church to have a department for local missions as to have a department for the Juniors? Surely the responsibilities of a church extend not only to those in the shadow of the church building, but to any and all unchurched communities in the association or even beyond the limits of the association.

Because of the importance of this work, the strongest, most compassionate man in the church should be superintendent of the mission department. The superintendent of the Junior department would be expected to organize enough classes for Juniors to enlist and minister to all the boys and girls in the community. Likewise, the superintendent of the mission department would be expected to guide the church in the organization of enough new work stations to minister to all the people in the association and beyond.

## III. Branch Stations Are Our Easiest Way to Enrol Many Lost People Immediately

New Sunday schools grow at the rate of about 65 for the first year. Therefore 10,000 new Sunday schools would increase our present enrolment by 600,000 and over within a year's time.

Dr. W. O. Vaught, Jr., pastor of the Immanuel Baptist Church, Little Rock, Arkansas, states:

"In our nine branch stations (six are now churches) there are more than 1,300 enrolled in Sunday school, and more than 900 enrolled in Training Union. In eight years, more than 500 have come through these arms for baptism. In my judgment this is the best plan for reaching the unreached multitudes."

## IV. Branch Stations Are Our Quickest Way to Win Large Numbers of People to Christ

New churches win people faster. The ratio of baptisms to church members in Southern Baptist churches is an average of one baptism for every twenty church members. In new churches the ratio is about one to six for the first two or three years. Ten thousand new churches organized now would provide an immediate soul-winning opportunity of 100,000 to 200,000 in numbers. That would be in addition to the opportunities in the present churches.

Dr. C. C. Warren, pastor of the First Baptist Church, Charlotte, North Carolina, says:

"For over twenty-five years I have received some of my greatest thrills in blazing new trails (starting new work). Last year 43 per cent of our additions by baptism came through sponsored chapels."

## V. Branch Stations Are an Effective Way to Develop a Missionary Spirit in the Present Churches

Dr. W. A. Criswell, pastor of the First Baptist Church, Dallas, Texas, testifies:

"When our First Baptist Church in Dallas began its Sunday school mission program, I was surprised at a reward that came in an altogether different place.

"When we established the Sunday schools, I was thinking only in terms of ministering to those untaught people. To my surprise, I found that the greatest reward was received in our own membership. The enterprise blessed our deacons, it blessed our home school, and it blessed our entire church.

"I can truthfully say that however much good we might be able to render those who attend our mission

Sunday schools, the greatest good is wrought here in our home church."

Dr. William D. Wyatt, pastor of the First Baptist Church, Albuquerque, New Mexico, out of his experience, says:

"Launching a new mission, and giving some of the church's best blood to man it, will put new life and vigor into the mother church every time. Our church has tested and proved this truth every year for several years."

## VI. The Present Churches Cannot Bring the People in the Unchurched Communities into Their Present Church Buildings

The existing churches can fill the present church buildings with the people who, in one way or another, are now connected with the present Sunday school enrolment and the resident church membership.

The distance prohibits any mass attendance of people in the unchurched communities in the existing churches. It is true that a few interested families may attend the existing churches, but the lost people and indifferent people will not attend. Busses may serve a temporary good to a few in these unchurched communities, but there is no permanency in the use of busses for this purpose. You do not change communities permanently by transporting a few people back and forth to a Sunday school outside the community. Every community needs a Baptist church. A new church in the community gives the people a church home all their very own.

## VII. The Need Cries Loud for Immediate Action

The establishment of branch stations in the right places in the right way at the right time with the right leaders by the right churches will have good success.

A new Sunday school is just another Sunday school exactly like the one in your present church building. One day somebody organized this Sunday school you now have. It may have been started in a home or a rented building. Some church may have erected a building for the new Sunday school. A superintendent was elected by your church to look after the new work. He was likely one of the deacons. This superintendent, along with your pastor, enlisted teachers.

One day the Sunday school was organized with six or more classes. On the very first day after the Sunday school, plans for preaching services were arranged by your pastor and the superintendent. On Sunday evening a Training Union was organized. This was followed by the preaching service. On Wednesday evening there was the prayer meeting. On Thursday a visitation program was initiated.

The work grew. After a few months a church was organized. Today you have a church home. Your family has a church home because somebody started a new work.

Will you provide a new work in some community so that in the other years there will be a church home for other people?

The Lord looked on the condition of the world and cried, "Whom shall I send, and who will go for us?" Isaiah answered, "Here am I; send me." Just as the community in Macedonia waited for Paul and his colaborers to come with the gospel message, so do thousands of communities all over our Convention territory wait for some church to come and provide Bible study and preaching services. Paul responded immediately to the Macedonian cry for help. There were difficulties far beyond the power of our imagination to visualize, but Paul and his faithful fellow laborers heard the cry, faced the dangers, sang and prayed in time of hardship, and, in spite of opposition, planted Bible-teaching stations for the Christ they loved in the communities that had called to them.

Who will make a motion that your church establish a department of local missions to work with the department of associational missions? Every church can have one or more branch stations.

Dr. Allen W. Graves, pastor of the Immanuel Baptist Church, Tulsa, Oklahoma, has led this good church to show us the way to enrol the multitudes for Bible study and thus win them to Christ. "We have established five new missions, four of which have become strong, thriving churches. We believe that the best way to advance the kingdom of God is to build strong, sound, co-operating, mission-minded Baptist churches in every community where a church is needed."

### Questions for Review

1. State seven imperative reasons why Southern Baptists must go into unreached communities with branch stations.
2. What department should every church set up to meet the needs of unreached communities?
3. What blessings come to the mother church because of opening new stations?

# 7. PASTORS MUST LEAD IN A CHURCH PROGRAM OF EVANGELISM

The primary functions of a church are: winning to Christ, world missions, enlisting in service, preaching, praying, teaching, training, giving, and singing. A church has units of work that are used to carry out these functions. One function can be carried out most effectively through one unit, and another function through another unit. Each function, however, is a church function, and each unit of work is a church unit. In this way all the church members work in all the church units for the purpose assigned by the church.

A brief study of the Southern Baptist church program of evangelism is presented.

## I. A Church Program of Evangelism

Southern Baptists have a church program of evangelism. The program is led by the pastor and carried out primarily through three of the church units of work. These three units of work are: the regular preaching services, the special revival meetings, and the Sunday school. It is participated in by members of every unit of work in a Baptist church. This program is practical, permanent, adequate, and resultful. It is church-centered and church-directed. It is inclusive, including all church members and all church units of work.

Some people may not understand how the program works, because they do not understand how a Baptist church works. A Baptist church has a number of units of work, and all the members of a church work through all the units provided for them for the accomplishment of different phases of the work. Under the leadership of the pastor all the members work through one unit for the accomplishment of one objective and through another unit for the accomplishment of another objective, but it is all church work and all for full New Testament evangelism.

A Baptist church has a preaching program. It is central in a Baptist church, and all other units support this ministry. The preaching program, however, is not the church. It is one of the chief functions of the church.

Evangelism is a major function of the preaching program. It is not the only function or purpose of the preaching program, but the preaching program, with both saved and unsaved people in attendance and with the gospel message, is permanent, practical, and resultful in evangelism. The regular preaching services are essential in evangelism, but they are not enough.

A Baptist church has a prayer program. It is usually conducted by the pastor. It is the prayer program of the church. The prayer meeting is not designed for a great evangelistic service nor for the most effective co-operative personal program of evangelism. It is a church in prayer, undergirding all its activities by drawing on divine resources of wisdom and power.

A Baptist church has a program of special revival, evangelistic efforts. While there are other purposes in special evangelistic efforts, the primal purpose is the harvest of souls. Every unit of a Baptist church participates in a revival. The special revivals are essential in a complete program of evangelism, but not enough.

A Baptist church has a financial program. The annual budget may be made out by a budget committee, adopted by the church conference, taught by the

Training Union, the Woman's Missionary Union, the Brotherhood, and the Sunday school. The offerings may be gathered in the Sunday school classes, but it is the financial program of the church. It is recognized by all church members as such. The financial program is essential in evangelism, but it is not in itself the means for enrolling lost people, promoting Bible study, and directing personal work.

A Baptist church has a music program. It is usually conducted by the minister of music and led by the choir. It is participated in by every member of the church and by all who attend any of the church units. The music program makes invaluable contributions to evangelism but not as an organization for soul-winning. The choir members engage in personal visitation but not in their capacity as singers. They are workers and members in the Sunday school, and their personal work for soul-winning is more effective if done through the classes and groups.

A Baptist church has a program of world missions. Its major purposes are instruction and enlistment in missions. All the women of the church find a major opportunity to study the mission work and to participate in mission causes through the Woman's Missionary Union. All units of church work teach, enlist, and support the missionary program of a church. The preaching service, the Training Union, and the Sunday school make major contributions to missions. This is evangelism in every sense of the word, but it is not primarily the organized effort of the church to find, bring in, win, and enlist every lost person in the church community.

A Baptist church has a church program of enlistment. The official aim of the Brotherhood is complete enlistment of all the men in the total church program. While all the church units make contributions in the task of enlistment, it is the chief function of the Brotherhood.

A Baptist church has a program for training church members. It is implemented through the Training Union, but it is the church program of training. The Training Union trains in personal development, personal soul-winning, missions, Bible study, giving, and service. The Training Union is no more an agency or auxiliary of the church than is the Sunday evening preaching hour or the music program. The Training Union is the church program of training for all church members in all the things a church does.

Enlistment and training are essential to evangelism, but it is imperative that a church shall have one unit which furnishes the channel through which enlisted, trained church members can work most effectively in winning the lost.

A Baptist church has a Bible-teaching program. It is channeled through the Sunday school. While all the church units of work study the Bible and use the Bible, yet the Sunday school is regarded by a church as the major means of providing regular Bible study for all the people. The Sunday school is no more an auxiliary to the church than the Sunday morning preaching services or the revival meetings. The Sunday school is the church at work in certain well-defined fields.

All these units make up the total church program of work: preaching, worship, teaching, missions, training, finance, enlistment, evangelism, prayer, and giving. While each unit has a distinctive function, yet the members of a church participate in all the units of work, and in that way all the church members have a part in all the work of the church.

## II. Why a Church Uses the Sunday School in Evangelism

All the people consider the preaching services and the revival meetings as essential in evangelism, and that is correct. We come now to see why a church will find it effective to major on the Sunday school as a unit for evangelism.

The majority of new church members come out of the Sunday school enrolment. In churches that have growing Sunday schools, the percentage runs about 90 per cent. In churches that do not have growing Sunday schools, the percentage is lower and the number of baptisms fewer.

The constituency of the Sunday school includes the unsaved as well as the saved, the children, boys and girls, as well as the adults. A major function of a church through the Sunday school is to enrol all the lost people in Sunday school for Bible study and for attendance in the preaching services.

The Sunday school provides regular Bible study for all the people. The program of Bible study includes the Sunday morning periods, the Vacation Bible school each year, the daily home study, and the January Bible Study Week. Bible study prepares individuals for conversion. Bible study leads to Christian living and service.

The Sunday school officers and teachers come from every unit of work in a church. Among them are members and workers in the Training Union, the Woman's Missionary Union, the Brotherhood, and the choir. Some are deacons and members of the special committees. All find in the Sunday school an effective channel for their evangelistic efforts.

The Sunday school constituency is graded into small groups by ages, where personal attention can be given on the level of the experience and needs of the individual.

The Sunday school meets immediately before the Sunday morning preaching hour, and the church uses the Sunday school to bring in the lost people and put them into the preaching service.

A Sunday school can be used to provide a church with a permanent, fruitful, soul-winning field. This can be done by enrolling the children while they are young and holding them in Sunday school until they reach the years of accountability.

The people who are in the Sunday school have studied the Bible and come to the preaching hour with the Word of God warm and powerful in their hearts.

The Sunday school provides a harvest of souls for the special revival meetings.

The pastor and church can use the Sunday school as often as needed in a soul-winning program of visitation. Since the Sunday school organization is made up of deacons, of workers and members of the W.M.U., the Training Union, the Brotherhood, and choir, the church is united in a soul-winning program of visitation in the church unit where the lost people are. Soul-winning visitation can be made more effective, more inclusive, and more permanent by use of the Sunday school than in any other known way.

Every week workers in the different units visit for expansion, for regular attendance, in ministry to sick members, to church members, and for many other purposes. Because the lost people are enrolled in the Sunday school and the members of all the units are mobilized for soul-winning, the church can go afield through the Sunday school, as often as is needed, in a united effort for personal soul-winning. Thus the Sunday school offers the channel for every member of every unit to put into practice the evangelism to which every unit is contributing.

Some churches select a small number of individuals and commit the soul-winning to them. This group goes by different names, sometimes known as the "Andrew Band." This plan is often called the soul-winning program of the church. Some of the evident weaknesses of this type of program are: it lacks permanency—the plan seldom lasts very long; it includes only a few of the church members; it by-passes all the regular units of a church, although the members of this band are usually workers selected from the regular units of the work of a church. This weakens the permanent church units and dissipates the effectiveness of the workers.

### III. Soul-winning Results Determined by the Way the Sunday School Is Used

Here are two groups of churches. Conditions are similar in the communities where these churches are located. One group has an average of 125 persons in Sunday school for every 100 church members. The other group has an average of 45 persons in Sunday school for every 100 church members.

The first group of churches reported one baptism for every thirteen church members in 1953. The second group reported one baptism for every fifty-two church members in 1953. Here again we see that Sunday school enrolment does have a favorable bearing on the number of baptisms in a church.

An increase in baptisms is not all. In the first group of churches there are approximately 30 Sunday school workers for every 100 church members. In the second group there are about 15 Sunday school workers for every 100 church members. The number of Christians put to work per church in each group of churches is what makes the difference in the Sunday school enrolment. The Sunday school enrolment makes the difference in the number of baptisms.

There is still another important difference. The first group of churches have twice as many people giving now as they had five years ago. Churches of the second group have only about 10 per cent more people giving now than five years ago. The average per capita gifts in the first group of churches is about the same as in the second group. The difference then is in the number of people giving in each group. It is significant to note that the new people average as much per capita as that given by the members who have been in the churches for more than five years.

## IV. Testimonies from Successful Churches

Two pastors from two different states bear testimony of the effectiveness of the Sunday school in winning people to Christ. First, here is a testimony from Dr. E. Hermond Westmoreland, pastor of the South Main Baptist Church, Houston, Texas:

"For several years our church has been listed among those baptizing more than 100 persons each year. Fully one third of these have been Adults. Nine out of ten of those reached have been reached through the Sunday school.

"Experience has proved that adults can be reached for Christ if they can be enlisted for Bible study. The Holy Spirit uses the truth of God's Word as an instrument to bring conviction of sin, to encourage faith, and to work the miracle of regeneration. It is the 'truth as it is in Christ Jesus' that produces the desired result.

"Most adults who have not been reached have been

denied instruction in God's Word in their youth. They are not given to individual study of the Bible or to regular attendance upon the preaching service. Our greatest hope of reaching them for Christ rests in the opportunity to reach them through a Sunday school class. It is my honest conviction that the small class will be more conducive to winning adults, since responsibility is more definitely placed, and concern for the individual is more evident than in the larger class.

"Given the opportunity to study the Word under the guidance of a consecrated teacher, warmed by the spiritual fellowship of an eager group of fellow class members, encouraged to attend worship services, the result is almost inevitable—they will be won to Christ."

Here is a testimony from John Buell, pastor of the Highlands Baptist Church, Highlands, North Carolina. It reveals very clearly that a Sunday school in a town where the people are very conservative can be made to grow and produce fruit.

"The enrolment of our Sunday school the first Sunday in October, 1953, was 176. It was 448 on March 1, 1954, just five months later. This is a net gain of 272 in five months.

"Several things have contributed to this growth. We moved up from a class Sunday school to a department Sunday school. This was an advance from eleven classes to thirty classes. A training program adopted in June, 1953, led to the study of seven books in the eight-month period. By March 1, forty of our workers had earned the Sunday School Worker's Diploma.

"Our objective is to have eighty of our workers who have earned this diploma by the close of the Sunday school year, when we will observe our annual commencement program and recognize those who have studied at least four books during the year.

"We adopted a visitation program and have followed it carefully. We have applied the laws of growth as found in the book *The Pull of the People,* and discovered that they will bear good fruit wherever they are put to use.

"We have every reason to believe we will reach our goal of 506 by the close of the associational year.

"In the five-month period, October, 1953 through February, 1954, the church received 45 people upon profession of faith. A total of 70 people joined the church during this period. We baptized 35 people during the week we studied *The Pull of the People.*"

## V. Some Things Accomplished Better by Use of the Sunday School

Pastors are busy men. Multitudes of demands are made upon them. Many duties call for the use of every hour of each day. It is not easy for a pastor to decide how best to use the time. If we take seriously the records in the churches and the testimonies of pastors, we are compelled to admit that time spent in building and using a Sunday school produces desired results beyond those produced in other ways.

Jesus, when on earth, faced the same situation as faced by many pastors of today. One evening, he went home with Peter. The people of the community came bringing their sick and lame, and Jesus healed them.

Next morning, Jesus arose early and slipped away to commune with his Father. He no doubt knew the people would return early with perhaps the request that he stay with them, so that their sick would be made well, their pantries always full, and their physical lives be made easy and pleasant. When Peter and the other disciples found Jesus and urged him to go back, he replied, "Let us go into the next towns, that I may preach there also: for therefore came I forth."

The people wanted one kind of ministry—physical comforts and physical luxuries. Jesus came to bring another kind of ministry—to seek and to save that which was lost. Before he returned to the Father, he told his disciples, "As my Father hath sent me, even so send I you."

Pastors today believe their work is exactly what Jesus commanded. The important question is to find the most effective way to carry out the work of Jesus—to turn people to Christ and help Christians grow up into him in all things "unto the measure of the stature of the fulness of Christ," even until they arrive at full maturity. The point here is that a church can win more people to Christ by the use of the Sunday school than by any other way, or combination of ways, now known. What are some things a church can do better by the use of the Sunday school?

Churches can enlist people by the use of the Sunday school. Churches can enrol people for Bible study at the rate of ten for every worker enlisted and trained. Arthur Flake discovered this law in 1919. Records show that this ratio has remained about the same all these years. It is a known fact, attested by years of experience in all our churches, that our Sunday schools enrol people just as fast as workers are enlisted and trained and space is provided for the needed departments and classes.

When a church has a growing Sunday school, more people are won to Christ. The more rapid the growth of the Sunday school, the greater will be the number of people won to Christ. The rapid growth of a Sunday school nearly always increases the efficiency in the work of a church. The training and organization necessary to produce the growth likewise increase the efficiency.

Churches that have 125 in Sunday school for every 100 church members report per capita gifts for Sunday school enrolment as large as reported in the churches that have 50 in Sunday school for every 100 church members.

So it is with giving money or any other line of work in a church. The way of progress is not fewer but more—more workers, more people, more soul-winning, more training, more regular giving. That is the way taught by Jesus. "The harvest truly is plenteous, but the labourers are few; pray ye therefore the Lord of the harvest, that he will send forth labourers into his harvest." So our prayers, coupled with our programs and our efforts, must be more, not less.

In some Sunday schools the major effort is on the attendance of the ones enrolled. That is good, but if followed to the neglect of the enlistment of new members, it leads to loss and not increase. Such a trend works in reverse. Efforts are centered in a high percentage of the enrolment in attendance. If that is all that is done, classes soon become crowded, groups in Adult classes become full. The result is that the visitation program is limited to the members of the class, and the class members find themselves visiting with each other. Then begins an endless circle of visiting absentees, who ought to be enlisted to visit and win new members and win lost people.

Right at this point is one of the chief reasons for keeping departments, classes, and groups small enough so that there is always room for others and a strong incentive to enrol and win others. Two other major reasons for this are to make possible individual participation and to provide good teaching and learning situations.

### VI. The Word "Must" in the Title

Look back now at the word "must" in the title of this chapter. What does it mean? It does not mean that any individual or any Convention agency may tell a pastor what he is to do. It does mean that pastors who desire these out-beyond results must build and use the Sunday school. Pastors must learn to make the Sunday school grow. They must learn how to relate properly the Sunday school to the total church program. They must select, train, and use large numbers of the church members as workers in the Sunday school. They must have a balanced development in Sunday school enrolment and attendance. The young people and adults must be in the Sunday school in large numbers.

A pastor is not compelled by force, coercion, conformity, or any other outward means to do these things. The point is, if he wants to enjoy these extra, out-beyond results, he must do these things. In the majority of cases, if the ratio of baptisms to church members is changed favorably, from one to forty to one to twenty, or from one to twenty to one to eight, then these things must be done. The decision rests at the point of the pastor's wanting these extra results enough to be willing to see that the things are done that will produce the extra results.

### Questions for Review

1. What units function in a church program of evangelism?
2. Through which unit of the church program can all the members of the church most effectively channel their soul-winning efforts?
3. What are some results in evangelism which can be accomplished better by the use of the Sunday school than through any other unit?

# 8. SUNDAY SCHOOL OFFICERS MUST PLAN WELL

"Why is Broadview Sunday School twice as large as ours? There are as many people in our community as in Broadview community." The question asked one evening in a workers' council caused those who were present to think, and the thinking resulted in change—change to some things that were being done at Broadview. The changes resulted in Sunday school gains. The enrolment gains resulted in a like increase in attendance, which resulted in more people added to the Lord and his church.

The Sunday school officers made the difference in the two churches. When the officers in the second Sunday school changed their attitudes and plans, the Sunday school was immediately changed from a static condition to a growing condition. The increase in attendance increased the soul-winning opportunities.

## I. Sunday School Officers Determine the Number of Baptisms

Sunday school officers, general, department, and class can, by the kind of plans they project for the Sunday school, create a condition that results in more people brought to Jesus. By their neglect and complacency Sunday school officers may, and often do, keep lost people away from Jesus.

The Sunday school officers determine the objective of the Sunday school. They decide the pattern of the organization and also the size of the organization. The intensity of spirit in the Sunday school moves up or down to the level of the spirit of the leaders. By the plans and programs they make they decide the quality of work done in a Sunday school. They can receive adequate help in all these important matters, but they determine whether they will receive the help, appropriate it, apply it, use it, and benefit from it.

The officers determine the rate of growth in a Sunday school. No other group can do this. The Sunday school officers are at the head of the procession, and the Sunday school moves along at the same rate of speed as the officers move.

The officers determine, more than any other group, the number of baptisms in a church. Not the teachers but the officers set the pace in evangelism. The teachers do much of the work, but the officers determine the conditions under which the teachers work. It is next to impossible to have uniformly good teaching in a Sunday school without good leadership on the part of the officers. It is most unusual to have personal soul-winners in a Sunday school unless the officers set the example.

The officers determine the number of Christian homes in a community. They do this by the provision made for the enrolment, attendance, teaching, and participation of the married young people and the adults and their children.

The officers determine the amount of money given as they determine the growth of the Sunday school, because new people brought in soon give as much per capita as those already enrolled.

The Sunday school officers do these things because of their positions. Along with the pastor, the educational director, the superintendent, the department superintendent, and the class officers determine the progress, attitudes, conception, and spirit of a Sunday school.

The work of a Sunday school always reflects the attitudes, conceptions, and energies of the officers.

The Sunday school will be what the officers make it, and it will do what the officers desire and plan for it to accomplish. The pastor and the other officers finally determine the place and use of the Sunday school in winning people to Christ.

A digest of two reports recently received reveals why some Sunday schools grow faster, do better work, and win more people than some others.

The first report shows the following spirit and lack of progress: "Our people were so busy that we did not study *The Pull of the People* last September. As April is such a busy month in our community, we voted last night that we would not observe April as Half-Million Month, but would leave the visitation to the classes to do the best they can. Our Sunday school enrolment is 32 less than the number reported to the association last September. We had so many members who had not been present for six Sundays or more that we decided to drop their names from our class rolls. Because of lack of space, we did not start any additional departments or classes at promotion time. We need more space, but some of our men feel that is not the time to build. Our Sunday school is doing good work, even though we do not show an enrolment increase. We wish *you* success in the 'Million More in '54' crusade."

The second report contained the following: "Last September we spent $3,000 and put three departments in the basement of the pastor's home next door to our church building. This enabled our Sunday school to move up from a class school to a department school. The enrolment the first Sunday in October was 176. It was 427 by February 1. We have 135 people in the three departments in the pastor's home. We will be compelled to erect a new educational building right away.

"Several things have contributed to this growth. The placing of the Sunday school on a department basis was perhaps the major factor. We went from eleven classes to thirty classes. We need six more now. We adopted a training program last June and have studied seven books during the past eight months. We have a regular plan of visitation. We have every reason to believe we will reach our goal of 506 total enrolment before the end of the Sunday school year. The co-operation of all our people is wonderful. We mailed our application for a Standard Sunday school last week."

These are statements lifted from two actual reports received the same day. The difference in Sunday schools is not determined by location or conditions, but by the officers. When Sunday school officers plan well, plan the work in the right way, the Sunday school does grow. This growth provides a church with opportunities to increase the number of baptisms, the number of regular givers, the number of Christian homes, the size of the Sunday morning preaching congregation, and other fruits that come from Bible study when every member of the family is in Sunday school.

Would you like to see a Sunday school in action in evangelism?

The revival meeting was three months away. The pastor and superintendent asked all officers and teachers to check the Sunday school rolls and list the names of all lost people. All of them were surprised and disturbed. Only a very few lost people were found to be enrolled in the Sunday school. Most of these were nine- and ten-year Juniors and a few parents of Cradle Roll babies. What had happened? The lost people enrolled had been won to Christ.

What happened? Names of prospects were secured. A study revealed the need for a department for the fifteen- and sixteen-year Intermediates, one for the seventeen- and eighteen-year Young People, and one for the married Young People. A study of the groups in Adult and Young People's classes revealed that the groups had for some time been too large for any additional growth. Most of the classes had been visiting, but they were visiting each other.

What did this Sunday school do? A place was found, a superintendent and two teachers were enlisted, and a department for married Young People was started. When the revival meeting began, 24 people had been enrolled in the two classes. During the meeting eleven of these joined the church, six by letter and five upon profession of faith in Christ.

Other departments were organized. Several of the classes reorganized the groups, making six groups when there had been four. Names of prospects were assigned, and the visitation program was revived. The result was a gain of 3 Juniors, 19 Intermediates, 22 Young People, and 37 Adults, a total of 81 net gain in three months. Seventy-two of them were not members of that church. During the revival 56 of them did unite with that church. Others came later.

What happened in this church in this three-month period indicates the most effective church program of evangelism now known to the churches. It was led by the pastor. The task of having lost people and detached church members ready for decision when the revival came was carried out through the Sunday school. The Sunday school officers, teachers, and members were also deacons, members of the W.M.U., Brotherhood, Training Union, choir, and finance committee.

In the meetings of the W.M.U. the members prayed together for the revival. Reports were made of the growth in the Sunday school, and the members of the

W.M.U. were urged to give their best in visitation through the Sunday school. The same things were done in the Training Union, Brotherhood, and choir. The deacons in the regular deacon's meeting were urged to give their best in their Sunday school classes or other positions. The result was a church revival—more than 100 added by baptism and more than 40 by transfer of letter.

## II. A Condition That Can Be Changed

In the period 1946-1951 the average annual Sunday school enrolment gain for Southern Baptists was 302,954. This is an annual average gain of ten per church. Does that mean that all the 28,000 Southern Baptist Sunday schools increased in enrolment during the five-year period? Sad it is, but that is not what the reports show.

Mr. J. P. Edmunds, secretary of the Department of Survey, Statistics, and Information of the Sunday School Board, shows from the reports of the churches as recorded in the associational minutes that 6,139 Southern Baptist Sunday schools report losses in 1951 over 1946. Why? Is it permissible to ask some questions? Where were the superintendents? Where were the department superintendents? Where were the pastors? Where were the men? Where were the women? Why the loss in enrolment in five of the best years of Sunday school work in history as to growth?

Where are these Sunday schools located? They are from every section of the territory and represent every size of church. Mr. Edmunds finds the following conditions:

23.9 per cent of city churches reported losses
23.7 per cent of open country churches reported losses

18.6 per cent of town churches reported losses
17.9 per cent of village churches reported losses

The startling fact disturbs us, or does it—that 22.2 per cent of all Southern Baptist Sunday schools reported a loss in a five-year period? Are these losses necessary? Surely not, as 18,000 churches report Sunday school gains.

## III. Marvelous Gains in Some Churches

There is a most encouraging side to the record. It is that approximately 5,000 Sunday schools report an annual average of about 25 net gain per church for the five-year period. Another 5,000 report an annual average of about 20 per church. Another 8,000 report smaller gains. About 5,000 churches report about the same enrolment as reported five years ago.

Why the gains in some of the churches? We call some of the pastors and superintendents for testimonies.

Here is the testimony of Rev. Ernest B. Myers, pastor in Nashville, Tennessee:

"From October 4, 1953, to February 28, 1954, the Sunday school enrolment in Riverside Church grew from 319 to 465, and the attendance from 185 to 347. The weekly offerings increased from $290 to $665, the church membership increased from 309 to 370. During this period there were 67 additions to the church, or an average of 13 per month.

"Our Cradle Roll department has opened doors and hearts. On one Sunday we enrolled 24 babies. Immediately we made pictures on color slides of all these babies and showed them on Cradle Roll Night in the revival meeting. All the parents were present. Five of the parents joined the church.

"We organized three new Nurseries, a department for married Young People, several new classes for

Juniors and Intermediates and Adults. We have had a training school each month since October.

"We have a weekly meeting of the officers and teachers and a weekly plan of visitation. It took a few weeks for us to create a winning spirit, but now the people love the church and are happy in service. We expect the gains during the next few months to be better than for the past five months."

Dr. C. Y. Dossey, a member of the evangelistic staff of the Home Mission Board, gives the following testimony regarding his experience in First Baptist Church, Gulfport, Mississippi. This church has had a growing Sunday school for several years. The growing Sunday school makes possible a marvelous harvest of souls.

"In April, 1952, I was in a revival in the First Baptist Church in Gulfport, Mississippi. During the revival we had 147 additions to the church, with over 100 of these coming by baptism. About 65 per cent of this number were adults. The First Baptist Church had two Adult departments at that time. On the middle Sunday morning we had an evangelistic service in the Sunday school, and many of the adults who were not Christians or church members were won. Every night the second week of the revival we had 'Sunday School at Night.' The entire Sunday school met before the evening preaching service. The Adult teachers met with their classes, and with the help of the saved members of their classes they were able to win almost every unsaved and unchurched member of the two Adult departments to Christ and the church. The Adult department of the Sunday school can be used to great advantage in winning the unsaved and unchurched to Christ and the church."

The achievements in the First Baptist Church of Whitesburg, Kentucky, reveal something of what is possible in any church. This church is located in the heart of the mountains of East Kentucky. The record of this church is given because the gains were made under all the usual difficulties known to churches in towns, villages, and open country.

In October, 1951, the Whitesburg Church had 178 enrolled in Sunday school in nineteen classes and eight departments. In addition, the church was conducting two branch stations with 122 enrolled.

In February, 1954, this church had 576 in the home church Sunday school in forty-two classes with 73 workers. At the same time this church was conducting six branch stations with 315 enrolled in twenty-one classes.

In two and one-half years this church has increased the Sunday school enrolment by 398 in the home church and 193 in the branch stations.

## IV. The Laws of Growth Fruitful

In all these churches the leaders followed the laws of Sunday school growth. These laws are stated and explained in *The Pull of the People*. Thousands of Sunday school officers have used these laws and achieved unusual success. When the laws of nature are followed, all nature works in harmony. When Sunday school officers obey the laws of Sunday school growth, these laws work with them. When these laws are ignored, they work against those who ignore them.

Because the First Church, Tulsa, Oklahoma, has had good success as a result of following these laws of growth, the educational director, Henry E. Love, was asked to give a testimony. Here is it:

"In the First Baptist Church, Tulsa, Oklahoma, we have applied the laws of Sunday school growth, and, as expected, some wonderful things have happened.

*"The enrolment has increased in proportion to the workers.*

| *Year* | *Workers* | *Enrolment* |
|---|---|---|
| 1953 | 321 | 3,114 |
| 1954 | 429 | 3,645 |

"The increase in new workers came suddenly, largely as a result of Adult grading, and yet we can already see the ratio pattern adjusting itself.

*"Many classes have reached their maximum growth in a few months after their beginning.*

"Five Adult classes doubled in enrolment in seven months. Many Junior and Intermediate classes increased from 6 and 7 to 10 and 12 members. From these, still other new classes were formed.

*"New units have grown faster, won more people to Christ, and provided more workers.*

"A separate department was provided for sixteen-year-olds at promotion. The seventeen-year group increased the following year from 48 to 81 members. When a department was provided for each year in the Intermediate section, the enrolment increased by 50.

"The Junior advance shows: 37 classes in 1953; 43 classes in 1954; enrolment, 348 in 1953; 399 in 1954.

"The Adult section has grown from 23 to 44 classes. What happened? Two hundred and twenty-five new Adults have been enrolled. Additions to the church through the Sunday school have doubled in the last year.

*"Grading by age has provided the logical basis for adding new working units.*

"In February, 1953, we completed the age grading of our entire Sunday school by age-grading Adults. This Christ-centered, church-centered program has solved more problems, reached more people, placed more workers in service, provided more effective Bible teaching than anything we have ever done in our school.

"One teacher, who formerly taught a class of 175 members, said, "After thirty years of trying, I feel that I am now really teaching for the first time in my life." On grading Sunday there were 21 members enrolled in his class. A few months later, this number had increased to 49.

*"Promotion recognizes the natural laws of growth and development.*

"We provide a central classification desk for new members and observe annual promotion of *all* age groups. Else, why grade? We still receive rich testimonies about our first Adult Promotion Day, especially concerning the more effective teaching, the new friendships, the privilege of studying with different teachers.

*"Enrolment and attendance have increased in proportion to the number of personal visits.*

"In February, 1954, our people made 2,195 personal visits. The average Sunday school attendance for the month was 1,913. In January, 1954, we made 1,978 personal visits. The average attendance was 1,792. When we average 2,000 visits a month, attendance remains high. When visitation lags, attendance drops.

"Our Sunday school enrolment has increased 531 during the last year, with an increase in average attendance of over 300. Visitation is the key!

*"The building sets the pattern.*

"In February, 1953, we entered our marvelous new, six-level educational addition. Space is provided for these departments: 7 Adult, 3 Young People, 4 Intermediate, 4 Junior, 4 Primary, 6 Beginner, and 8 Nursery.

"What has happened? The inevitable! We need more room!"

## V. Planning and Building Committees Limit or Extend Soul-winning Opportunities

Mr. Chairman of the Planning or Building Committee, the kind of church building you lead your church to erect will, in a very definite way, determine the number of baptisms year by year in your church in the years that are ahead. The type and size of building you lead your church to erect may not show a trend or change in baptisms the next year, but the trend will show very soon. This is true because the building determines the rate of growth in the Sunday school and the Sunday school gains and the number of baptisms go up and down together.

Quoting Mr. W. A. Harrell, secretary of the Department of Church Building and Church Architecture:

"It is the urgent business of winning people to Christ that makes a building important in the program of a church. People must be reached and taught God's Word. That takes a building. People respond and accept Christ under the influence of preaching. They must have a place to assemble for worship and preaching. That takes a building.

"The arrangement of the building has everything to do with the response. The auditorium should have a warm, friendly atmosphere with the pulpit as the central feature.

"It should be easy to see and hear and respond to an impulse to go forward. The auditorium that emphasizes the individual in seating arrangement, both on the main floor and in the balcony with steps leading directly to the main floor at the front, is an imperative and the desire of every evangelistic pastor.

"The educational building must not only provide for people, but it likewise must place emphasis on the individual. That is the reason for classrooms for all ages at least from Junior up and rooms that are not too large. A Sunday school class should be of such size that the teacher can give individual attention to each member. Therefore the building arrangement and provision are of utmost importance from the Nursery through the Adult departments.

"The building does and will help or hinder evangelism."

Dr. Donald F. Ackland contributes an important word as to the importance of the right type of church building:

"It will be no new thought to readers of the Bible that buildings may possess spiritual significances and be the interpreters of spiritual ideas.

"One result of present-day travel facilities is that on nearly every church building committee there is likely to be at least one person who will talk ecstatically about the artistic dignity and spiritual value of the ancient churches of Europe and their modern counterparts, with their divided chancels, central altars, and side pulpits.

"Is it possible that the advocates of this interior arrangement for Baptist auditoriums fail to realize that they are seeking to perpetuate a form which belongs to the years of ecclesiastical decadence and which maintains a symbolism cancelled at Calvary?

"It was no accident that our Baptist forefathers constructed their churches as auditoriums and not temples. Being men of keen theological vision and strong doctrinal conviction, they recognized the relevancy between the layout of the Christian auditorium and scriptural doctrine, and that while certain styles of architecture might meet the needs of Roman Catholicism and other sacramental bodies, they were not suitable for the worship of those who believe in a

Bible-centered ministry and the priesthood of all believers.

"A central pulpit and an open Bible place the emphasis where it should be—upon the revealed Word which at once inspires our worship, declares our doctrines, authenticates our ordinances, sustains our spiritual vigor, and points the way of life to sinful men.

"Our faith is evangelical, not sacramental; our worship is spiritual, not ritualistic; our ministry is ambassadorial, not sacerdotal.

"How important, then, that the places in which we gather to preach and praise and pray should be consistent with these glorious principles and express the concepts, not of unscriptural ecclesiasticism, but of Bible-based, Bible-centered, Bible-propagating Christianity, which exists to bear witness to the living Word in terms of the written Word."

The place of worship and preaching should be planned for evangelism. (The present trend to call the place of public worship and preaching "the sanctuary" may need some careful study.) The looks and designs of the place of public worship and preaching are certainly important. The first consideration, however, should be to bring people to Jesus. A second balcony may be necessary in some cases, but it is most difficult to get lost people to come out of a second balcony to make a public profession of faith in Christ and unite with the church. A place for preaching should place the people as near the preacher as is possible.

Mrs. Lillian Moore Rice, superintendent of Sunday school work with Juniors for Southern Baptists, out of her study, experience, and observation, expresses the position of Southern Baptist churches as to physical provisions in the church buildings for Juniors and Intermediates.

"A room for any group in the Sunday school should take its shape from the type of work and study carried on in that room. To decide what kind of rooms are right and good for Juniors and Intermediates we must decide what kind of Sunday morning program most effectively meets their growing needs.

"Juniors and Intermediates are old enough to use the Textbook of the Sunday school in their study. Sunday morning procedure for them, therefore, revolves around the study of the Bible. All the other teaching activities—map and picture studies, quizzes, discussions, pencil- and paper-work, problem-solving, thinking, choosing, deciding—are for the purpose of enriching Bible study, and helping the pupils relate its truth to their own lives.

"What type of room arrangement, then, best lends itself to serious study of the Bible? Juniors and Intermediates need classrooms where small groups of the same age may gather with Bibles in their hands to study, discuss, and think with the least possible distraction. That means classrooms with doors, and, if possible, with soundproof walls.

"There is a movement in some groups away from classrooms for Juniors. Instead, a large open room is provided for group activities. As I see it, this system has disadvantages for older boys and girls. In so many of our Baptist churches, the Junior groups are too large to function efficiently in this type of 'free' program. Under this system, too, the Junior misses one of the rich values of Sunday school—the close, week-by-week contact with one teacher, a teacher who loves him, who studies him as an individual, who knows his problems, cultivates his friendship, and stands by when trouble comes.

"Classrooms, then, seem to be the best answer to the question of right provision for Juniors and Intermediates in the Sunday school. Certainly these rooms should be large enough to prevent crowding and to permit freedom of movement."

Some professional architects and some independent advocates of church achitecture are calling our classrooms "cubbyholes." Some are saying that for the sake of symmetry and beauty and design, church buildings should not be so large. Some are advocating a Junior room, or a Primary room, or a Senior room.

These advocates are thinking in terms of 25 to 30 Juniors as the limit. Southern Baptists think and plan for all the Juniors and, of course, all other age groups. Southern Baptist churches are planning for and now have 200, 300, and up to 400 Juniors in one Sunday school. They have done this by creating buildings that accommodate four departments for Juniors, with 32 classrooms, or eight departments for Juniors with 64 classrooms.

When a church provides in the building a "Junior room"—one open room—it simply means that church does not have the conception of a Bible ministry, a soul-winning task, and a character building job which your church has.

What is the answer to those who call our classrooms "cubbyholes" and ask, "How can a church building be made beautiful when a hundred little rooms are demanded?" There are good reasons that make up the answer.

During the period 1940-1951 Southern Baptist Sunday schools showed a net enrolment gain of 46.3 per cent, while nine other leading denominations showed a net enrolment gain of 3.5 per cent. The Sunday school program of Southern Baptists, which demands a specific type of building, explains the difference in growth. An increase in enrolment means an equal increase in opportunity.

## VI. Educational Buildings of the Right Kind Are Wise Church Investments

The increase in attendance, which is always possible by increased space, soon pays for the building and then provides means for mission work of all types and in all areas of the earth.

Central Park Baptist Church, Birmingham, Alabama, discovered this fact, and for several years the church experienced a marvelous growth in attendance and a remarkable increase in baptisms.

In 1938 the first unit of a frame building was erected. In 1946 the second unit was added at a cost of $10,000. An investment of $10,000 has produced in fifteen years $115,189.98 in additional offerings.

In 1948 a building was secured at a cost of $11,000. This investment of $11,000 in four and one-half years produced $59,365.38.

Other investments in buildings for Sunday school and Training purposes have produced similar results.

This church recently secured an entire block on which are twelve residences. The cost was $160,000. The offerings from the increased attendance is more than sufficient to make the regular payments.

The Capitol Heights Baptist Church, of Montgomery, Alabama, erected a new educational building at a total cost of $103,000. As a result the Sunday school enrolment increased from 1,217 to 1,393, or a net gain of 176. The weekly offerings increased $1,411 or more than the monthly payments on the new building.

There is a direct relationship of room in a church building and the growth of the Sunday school. You have seen in the preceding seven chapters how Sunday school growth and the number of baptisms in a church move up and down together.

Salem Baptist Church in Alabama provided some

additional space, adjusted space that had not been fully used, and increased the Sunday school enrolment by 77. In 1946 the baptisms were zero; in 1953, nineteen.

South Main Baptist Church in Houston, Texas, erected a new educational building and as a result increased the Sunday school enrolment 30 per cent and the number of baptisms 65 per cent.

Any provision that increases the Sunday school enrolment makes possible an increase in the number of baptisms.

Let it be said that when the chairman of the Building Committee or the Planning Committee leads a church to erect a building that provides for a 50 per cent or a 100 per cent increase in Sunday school enrolment he has led the church to add proportionately to the soul-winning opportunity. Would it help to state it negatively? When the responsible people fail to provide for the growth of the Sunday school, they limit the soul-winning opportunities of the church.

## Questions for Review

1. Show the truth of the statement that Sunday school officers largely determine the number of baptisms which a church will have.
2. From the testimonies in this chapter, list the most effective things which have produced growth in Sunday school enrolment.
3. What is the testimony of the First Baptist Church, Tulsa, Oklahoma, as to the operation of the laws of growth in their situation?
4. What type of provision in the building has proved most fruitful for winning Juniors?

# 9. TEACHERS MUST WITNESS

Sunday school teachers are the most effective ready-to-be-used potential for soul-winning in all our Baptist life. It may be said with some truth that many of us have not been as faithful in personal soul-winning as our positions require. It may likewise be said that many Sunday school teachers have never been trained, encouraged, or led to be soul-winners.

Some may say that Sunday school teachers because of who they are should be good soul-winners without specific training. Would a general really expect a company of men to be good soldiers until they were trained, not only as individuals but as a group? The majority of men selected for military service make good soldiers when trained and led. Is it not just as true that Sunday school teachers make good soul-winners when trained and led? This does not mean that knowledge of technique is the only thing a soul-winner needs. Surely a knowledge of the Bible teachings about sin, salvation, God's promise to save all who will come to Jesus is essential. Study how Jesus dealt with people as they were, where they were. Is not this necessary knowledge? Jesus sent the seventy out with definite instructions that had taken months to impart.

What many churches have already done demonstrates that most churches could change the ratio of baptisms to church members by recognizing that the Sunday school teachers compose the most ready-at-hand, adequate, ever present, strategically placed group of workers a church has or can have and by using them to that end. They are members and workers in the W.M.U., the Training Union, the choir, the prayer meeting, the financial program, but they are better placed for soul-winning in the Sunday school than in any other unit of church work. They do other necessary phases of work through other church units and do them wonderfully well, but they do the work of personal soul-winning better through the Sunday school than in any other way.

## I. Teachers Must Witness

Royal words of assignment come from our Saviour and Lord—"Ye shall be witnesses unto me." Divine words of assurance accompany the words of assignment—"Ye shall receive power."

God desires to convince the people of the earth of his truth and mercy and to bring them to salvation. This he must do by human witnesses. "And ye shall be witnesses unto me" calls all Christians to the most important work ever committed to men, that of bringing people to Jesus.

While all true Christians must be witnesses, Sunday school teachers have a most natural, personal, sympathetic approach. The first approach is easy, natural, and attractive. It is an invitation, "Come study the Bible with us." This invitation is usually accepted if extended in love and supported by a good life. The invitation may need to be repeated, but when love prompts the repeated invitation, impressions are deepened. In this invitation a first step toward the salvation of a soul has been made.

It was Friday night of an eight-day revival. The brief gospel message had been delivered. The choir and the people were singing the invitation "Softly and Tenderly Jesus Is Calling." Down the side aisle came a Sunday school teacher and seven boys. No one was greatly surprised, though all were delighted. The man, a teacher of eleven-year-old boys, was a soul-winner every year. The pastor had trained him. Nine of the boys had been assigned to the teacher at promotion time. Five months had passed. Two of the boys were Christians, seven were not. The teacher had taught for their salvation. He had lived for their salvation. He had visited in the homes, talked and prayed with parents. He had consulted with the pastor and department superintendent.

During the first days of this week the teacher had been to see each of the seven boys. Two or three of them had already made profession of their faith in Christ. All were under conviction. The teacher, department superintendent, and parents had talked, prayed, and waited. When Friday came, all seven boys were Christians. The teacher, in co-operation with the parents, had made it possible for each boy to be present in the service and to make public profession of faith in Christ.

This man was a successful soul-winner because of the type of church program his church has. The pastor in seventeen years of service with these people had helped the church build a balanced church program. The W.M.U., the Training Union, the Brotherhood, the music, the prayer program, the financial plans were all of the best.

The preaching program was the center, and all the rest of the church program was built around this. The four annual revivals have been powerful influences in the church. The Sunday school is used as the unit that seeks primarily to enrol all the lost people for Bible study and the preaching hours. When they have been won to Christ, they are immediately led into active participation in all other units of work.

The pastor, more than any other individual, or any combination of individuals, has led in the development of the church program, has trained the officers and teachers in personal evangelism, and has kept them eagerly active in their assigned work.

Today this church has 1,623 church members, and 2,412 in Sunday school. During the past eighteen years the ratio of baptisms to church members which has been maintained in this church has been one to eleven.

In eighteen years this church has not been known to go around the Sunday school officers and teachers in any soul-winning effort of the church. The result has been a ratio of baptisms to church members of one to eleven over a period of eighteen years. Nearly a million Sunday school officers and teachers in Southern Baptist churches wait for the pastors and other leaders to build a church program of evangelism, train the Sunday school officers and teachers to be effective Bible teachers and successful personal soul-winners.

## II. The Teachers' Witness Essential and Effective

Teachers must be led to witness if the churches are going to win increasing numbers of people to Christ.

### 1. *Personal Relationship Vital*

The teacher can know the personal spiritual condition of each member of the class. A good teacher will seek lovingly to know and understand the problems and inner conflicts of each lost member of the class. The teacher usually understands the lost members of his class more thoroughly than any other member of the church, quite often more thoroughly than the parents in the home.

Several factors contribute to this helpful relationship. The first one is small classes, six to seven Juniors and Intermediates; ten to fourteen Young People; fifteen to twenty Adults. Such classes provide better soul-winning opportunities for a church, and certainly for the teachers.

Warm, personal contacts in social activities bring teacher and class members close together. A teacher sees all the life of a person in frequent social relationships. Fortunate is the teacher who has access to a car and can drive now and again through the quiet sections of a community with just one member of the class. A man twenty-seven years of age came forward for church membership on Sunday morning. The same afternoon his teacher said, "He made his decision Friday as we rode along in a quiet place."

There is nothing known that will take the place of personal visitation. Professional visits will do little if any good. Warm, personal visits, born and impelled by love and concern, will do good, and usually will win. Personal visits need not be long. Usually very brief visits are better. When need demands, longer personal visits may be necessary. It is necessary for the teacher to visit the member in his home. There can and should be many other visits. Invite the member to the home of the teacher. Provide transportation when needed.

Let the teacher develop and always manifest a warm, personal concern in and for the class member, and then the witness will be appreciated and effective. The teacher will take the advantage of every opportunity to know individual and group characteristics. Seek for knowledge about people and use the knowledge to be a more effective witness.

Mutual love between teacher and member provides an essential basis for good witnessing.

### 2. *Their Knowledge of Objectives and Methods by Age Groups Necessary*

The Cradle Roll visitor is a teacher, and when her work is done well she lays foundations for all future decisions. Sunday school classes for the fathers, classes for the mothers, Nurseries for the babies, places for the children as they become Beginners, and then Primaries, seek to prepare each child for early conversion.

When the church does the work well in the Cradle Roll, Nursery, Beginner, Primary, married Young People's departments, and the department for young Adults, the conversion of Juniors and Intermediates is almost 100 per cent.

Perhaps the greatest need now is for a better understanding of the purpose of grading and promoting of Young People and Adults, smaller classes, and the group plan of organization. The final purpose of it all is winning to Christ. Results in churches reveal the reasons for and the fruits of grading, promotion, small classes, and small groups.

Men and women have acute personality problems, and small classes and small groups enable teacher and group leaders to know the personal problems. When they know these things, it is much easier for them to help where help is needed.

### 3. *Their Intimate Contact with Home and Parents Invaluable*

The teacher's intimate contact with the home and the parents is invaluable in soul-winning. Here again we come face to face with the need for small classes and small groups. One visit each year into a home may be of some help, but not very much. One visit may give a teacher or a worker the wrong impression. You do not really know people unless you can be with them when they are relaxed. It takes time and repeated visits to know the parental attitudes, family customs, church relationships of each member of the family.

A surface knowledge may lead to a critical attitude. The many questions and critical feelings a teacher may have from a first visit may later turn to sympathy, and sympathy to compassion, and compassion to active, helpful, acceptable efforts. Know the heart problems, the family problems, the family relationship of wife and husband if you would help meet actual needs.

Teachers can link their class members to the pastor. The teacher can open the way for a well-timed visit from the pastor. One teacher, after she had done all she could to win her girls, went to her pastor and said, "You must go with me to see each one of the girls who is not a Christian." The result was that all her girls became Christians within a few weeks' period.

Teachers of boys and girls, and workers with babies and small children, can win parents to Christ. If their interest in the child is sincere and positive, the worker with the child will have one of the easiest approaches to the heart of the parent.

Often the workers with children can influence the parents to attend the Sunday school and preaching hours. There is always the opportunity to leave helpful literature in the home.

4. *Sunday Morning Offers Witnessing Opportunities*

There is every Sunday morning the opportunity for guided Bible study. When the teacher knows the condition and need of the class member, he can find in the Bible just the word that the Holy Spirit will use. The teacher's part is to know the need of the class members and the Word of God that will meet that need.

A mother will, under the directions of the doctor, tenderly give the child the medicine, and then wait prayerfully and eagerly for the medicine to do the work. Just so the teacher, under the direction of the

Holy Spirit of God, will give the Word of God to the sin-sick soul, and then pray and speak words of counsel and pleading, and let the Holy Spirit use the Word to do the work of God in the heart of the individual.

Teacher, remember it is God through Jesus Christ who does the saving. The Bible is the Word of God to bring the lost person to a realization of his need for a Saviour. The Holy Spirit helps him to repent and place his faith in Jesus. Thus the triune God, by use of the Word of God and the Christian's witness, brings men, women, boys, and girls into the kingdom of God, from death to life, from darkness to light, from waste to service. Remember, Bible teaching is your chief job.

Early moments on Sunday morning provide good opportunities for personal expression of interest. A word rightly spoken to an early-comer is powerful and will remain in the heart for weeks.

Preaching attendance is a major opportunity of the teacher. It is as essential to have the class members in the preaching hour as in the teaching hour. Both are essential. It is not one or the other, but both. Regular preaching attendance on the part of every member will require much personal work, often transportation provided after the preaching hour. Any effort necessary to have every member in the preaching hour is justified many times over in spiritual results.

5. *Watching for Timely Opportunities to Press for Decisions*

Careful, prayerful watching enables the teacher to press for a decision at the right time. Observation will reveal when impressions have been made. Then is the time to press for decision. It may be some real or imaginary difficulty that needs to be cleared up. It may be at a time when circumstances open the way for a decision.

A Cradle Roll visitor waited more than a year for a "right time" to press for a decision by father and mother. The circumstance arrived and the Cradle Roll visitor won the parents. A teacher waited three years for the right time to press for a decision. The time came when her neighbor was willing, even eager to listen.

6. *Opportunities for Co-operation in Other Church Units*

A teacher will see that new converts are immediately enrolled in the Training Union, and in the W.M.U., or the Brotherhood. The growth of the new Christian is essential, and Southern Baptist churches have a program for that purpose.

7. *Every Christian Class Member a Witness*

The teacher must seek constantly to develop every Christian member of his class to quickly become a personal soul-winner. The group plan in the Adult, Young People's, and Intermediate classes is ideal for developing witnesses. Lead the groups to make the enrolment and salvation of lost people the major task of the visitation program. Keep the groups small enough to encourage growth. Use *all* Christian class members to visit lost people and to witness. Do not permit a group or class to spend all the time visiting absentees when they should be put to work visiting unsaved people. See chapters 2 and 4 for a further discussion of the use of groups in evangelism.

## III. Provide Church Training Program for Stimulating and Training Teachers to Witness

In the churches is an army of officers and teachers waiting and ready to be trained in soul-winning.

We call Carl A. Howell, pastor of Murray Hill Baptist Church, Jacksonville, Florida, for testimony of what is possible when a church takes seriously the task of training the Sunday school officers and teachers for evangelism:

"Through the years we have expected our Sunday school officers and teachers to make winning to Christ the major purpose of all their work. This is true beginning with the Cradle Roll workers and continuing through the Extension department.

"Our general superintendent, J. B. Bagnal, Jr., is an effective personal soul-winner. He works at the task of personal soul-winning. He visits an average of twenty hours each week. He visits for many purposes, but all of it is ultimately for the purpose of winning people to Christ.

"Not all our 320 and more officers and teachers are active personal soul-winners. Many of them are. All of them, however, help make the Sunday school grow regularly, and this creates a soul-winning condition.

"Our Sunday school workers are faithful in attendance, loyal to the preaching services, and true to their assigned tasks. Our Sunday school workers, including all our class officers, provide our church with an adequate, practical, workable means of winning people to Christ under the most favorable conditions.

"We hold frequent training schools. We have a regular meeting of our officers and teachers. We take our workers to Ridgecrest and to our state Sunday school meetings. We urge our workers to attend the associational Sunday school conferences. They respond wonderfully well, and the results justify all our efforts."

The assertion is often made: Whatever you want to have in your Sunday school, train for it. Does your church really desire a band of witnessing, soul-winning teachers? Train for it.

Relate your training program to the needs of your group. Make careful study of the curriculum outlined in the Sunday School Training Course, and plan for a balanced course in your church this year. Include some of the excellent books on personal soul-winning from the Training Union Study Course.

Training teachers to witness in the fullest sense of the word includes training them in the technique of soul-winning and in the skills needed for effective Bible teaching. It also includes enriching their Bible knowledge and deepening their own spiritual lives. It includes helping them to a better understanding of their pupils, and of how the entire administrative program contributes to evangelism.

When the church calendar of activities is set up, see that the Sunday school training program is included. Workers are so busy that it is difficult to set any date which will suit them all for a training school. It will take frequent schools—perhaps one each month—to lead each worker each year to study four or more books in the Sunday School Training Course.

Make the most of training opportunities offered at Ridgecrest, Glorieta, and in Convention-wide clinics. Promote attendance on associational and group schools or clinics, on statewide assemblies, conventions, and clinics for Sunday school workers.

The outstanding opportunity for stimulating and training teachers to witness is through the weekly officers and teachers' meeting. This in-service program of training developed in Southern Baptist Sunday schools is the wonder and admiration of leaders in the educational world. More important to us, it is obedience to the scriptural injunction: "Consider one another to provoke unto love and to good works" (Heb. 10:24). It offers week-by-week opportunity to help each teacher plan to make the lesson presentation an effective witness to lost people in the class and a means of developing Christians as witnesses.

In the weekly officers and teachers' meeting assignments of prospects are made, and reports given about people won to Christ. This is an effective stimulation to the teachers to promote visitation and soul-winning in the class.

The achievement of everything which has been set forth in this book regarding the "how" of bringing more people to salvation and baptism depends on the right kind of workers. Securing the right kind of workers depends on a training program directed by the Holy Spirit.

## IV. Effective Places for Resultful Witnessing

Evangelism is more effective when woven right into the lesson for the day and when decisions are made in the classroom, in hallways, on way to preaching service, and in the preaching service.

Evangelism is resultful when something in the classroom, or the preaching service, or the visit reveals a "readiness" on the part of the class member, which is followed up immediately.

Evangelistic approaches are favorably received when the teacher utilizes opportunities which relate to special events in the pupil's life, such as a birthday, Promotion Day, graduation, going away to college, marriage, coming of the first baby, moving into a new home, promotion at place of work, or death of a loved one.

Yes, teachers, officers, class officers, and class members can be trained and led in a church program of soul-winning. Most of them will respond. They wait for church encouragement, training, and examples of leaders.

## Questions for Review

1. Which group of workers in the church are potentially the most effective soul-winners?
2. Make seven statements to show why and how the teachers can be the most effective soul-winners in a church.
3. How can a church train and lead its teachers to become effective in the church program of soul-winning?